God So Loved the World...

That He Created Chocolate

52 Fun and Inspiring Devotions For Women

Group

Loveland, Colorado

God So Loved the World...
That He Created Chocolate

52 Fun and Inspiring Devotions For Women

Visit our website: **group.com/women** and **girlfriendsunlimited.com**

Credits

This book was written by women who are part of Girlfriends Unlimited. Each author's name is included with the devotion she wrote.

Executive Editor: Amy Nappa
Chief Creative Officer: Joani Schultz
Copy Editor: Janis Sampson
Print Production Artist: Shelly Dillon
Art Director and Book Designer: Samantha Wranosky
Illustrator: Kadence Ainsworth
Production Manager: DeAnne Lear

Unless otherwise indicated, all Scripture quotations are taken from the *Holy Bible,* New Living Translation, copyright © 1996, 2004. Used by permission of Tyndale House Publishers, Inc., Carol Stream, Illinois 60188. All rights reserved.

Library of Congress Cataloging-in-Publication Data

    God so loved the world that he created chocolate : a devotional by girlfriends for girlfriends.

      p. cm.

    ISBN 978-0-7644-6666-3 (pbk. : alk. paper)

1. Christian women—Prayers and devotions. 2. Female friendship—Prayers and devotions. 3. Cookery (Chocolate)

    BV4844.G635 2010

    242'.643—dc22

    ISBN 978-0-7644-6666-3

10 9 8 7 6 5 4 3 2   19 18 17 16 15 14 13 12 11
Printed in the United States of America.

Table of Contents

Table of Contents, cont.

Table of Contents, cont.

God Loves You, Girlfriend!

"For God loved the world so much that he gave his one and only Son, so that everyone who believes in him will not perish but have eternal life." (John 3:16)

This verse is so much what we are about. Sharing God's love. Sharing the good news about that love. Sharing the joy of knowing we can have eternal life with God because of the gift of God's Son. As women, that also means sharing our lives…and a little bit of chocolate.

This book is about celebrating God's love and the relationships we can have because of that love. Relationship with God. Relationships with family. Relationships with friends—especially girlfriends! We asked women around the world to share their stories with us, and the result is this book. Women sharing their hearts, stories, and their journeys with one another.

There are 52 devotions in this book, enough to last you a year if you only read one a week (but we won't discourage you from reading them as quickly as you want!). Each includes a Bible passage and a reading, as well as a "Sweeten Your Life" idea to put what you've read into action right away. These are super-simple suggestions that anyone can do—even you!

And mixed in with these devotions, you'll find "God Loves Girlfriends" pages, which will help you discuss with other women what you're learning through these devotions. You can use these when you get together with a friend for coffee or any time you get together with a group of women.

These extra "God Loves Girlfriends" pages will help you share what's happening in your life through using this book. So be sure that all your friends have a copy of this book so discussion of these devotions can happen easily and naturally. No matter where you are in the book, you can share by using the suggestions on these pages.

And then, tucked in here and there, you'll find a few delicious (and super-easy) recipes for chocolate treats. Make these with your friends, make them for your friends, eat them with your friends. You get the idea!

So celebrate God's love. Celebrate friendships. And celebrate chocolate!

"Taste and see that the Lord is good."
(Psalm 34:8)

Chocolate Words

Kind words are like honey—sweet to the soul and healthy for the body.
(Proverbs 16:24)

My friend Patty is a traveler. She heads off on an airplane just about every weekend to some new experience. Instead of being jealous though, I'm always glad she's hitting the road. Why? She always brings back chocolates from afar! Sometimes they're strange chocolates with odd fillings like horseradish or a paste made from chili peppers. Other times there are tangy lemon fillings or dark, dark chocolate creams. It's an adventure for the taste buds!

When Patty gets back from one of her trips, those of us in the office gather around the new box of chocolates for a shared tasting experience. We look at the little "map" that tells what's inside each treat, make our choices, and then bite into these flavor-filled nuggets. We take time to savor the flavors and make suggestions to one another on which ones to try next. It's a fun ritual started because of Patty's sweet and generous heart.

Even sweeter than those delicious chocolates though, are Patty's words. She is one of those people who is generous with words of praise. Generous with her kind observations. Generous with sweet, sweet words that uplift, encourage, and bring joy. Everyone loves to be around Patty—not because she brings chocolate, but because she brings love.

In the Bible, sweet things are often associated with honey. I think that's because the people living in Bible times simply hadn't tasted chocolate yet. Honey was the sweetest thing they could use for comparison. So while it's certainly true that Patty's kind words are like honey, I prefer to think of them as chocolates for friends. Sweet to our souls and healthy for our bodies.

Amy Nappa

Sweeten Your Life

Pick up one or two chocolates for a girlfriend. Deliver them with a note filled with words of true kindness and encouragement for your friend. Let her know how God has used her in your life. Let her know the wonderful things you see in her. Fill her soul with sweet joy!

Thanks, Friend

My friend Tracie recently wrote me a letter. Not a brief thank-you note. This was a full-blown, handwritten letter. She said she wanted to put into writing several reasons she appreciates me as a friend. What a blessing! After reading her letter, I stopped to reflect on the reasons I appreciate our friendship.

Dependability. When Tracie and I set a meeting time and place, she's there. When she says she'll lend me a book, check a website, or confirm a date, she does it right away. Most of all, when she says she'll pray for me, I'm confident she does. She sends me a Facebook note or text message to remind me she's prayed and asks me for updates.

Generosity. It's not that Tracie gives me things (although she does). It's that she gives me herself. When we're together, she gives me her full attention. She shares her thoughts, passions, and everyday life with me. She regularly invests in our friendship.

Faithfulness. Tracie is a woman after God's heart. We attend different churches but meet regularly to study together and encourage each other. I can count on Tracie to hold me accountable, ask me the tough questions, and encourage me to make sound decisions.

Tracie's not perfect, and she'd be the first to admit it, but we both think we get the best end of our relationship. Perhaps you have a golden friendship. Or God might be providing you with several friends whose qualities combine to give you exceptional benefits of friendships. What do you value in your friendships?

Susan Lawrence

Sweeten Your Life

Consider three qualities you value in friendships. Who reflects (or has reflected) these qualities to you? Send a personal note to each precious girlfriend. Include a piece of chocolate to remind her of the sweet gift of friendship.

Great Expectations

And God will generously provide all you need. Then you will always have everything you need and plenty left over to share with others.
(2 Corinthians 9:8)

When I was expecting my daughter, Emma, I had some major complications and ended up on strict bed rest for six months. "Strict" meant limited movement and activity for three months, and then the following three months of it were "super-strict." I could only get up to use the bathroom!

I was already a mom to three other children, who needed me; and a wife to my husband, who, although helpful, had come to depend on me to manage our home. I was responsible for the cooking, cleaning, looking after the kids, and so on. We had to make some major adjustments. My husband had to learn how to cook and clean, and I had to learn to accept his way of cooking and cleaning! I realized I had taken my freedom for granted, and now that I had lost it, I was really missing it. This was difficult and frustrating!

Every morning my husband would get up and get our two oldest children ready for school and out the door after making a quick breakfast for me and leaving something in the fridge for my lunch. I felt so helpless, especially when he forgot the mayonnaise on my sandwich.

One day a friend came to visit me and brought me a journal. It had black pages with beautiful designs on the edge of each page. She also brought me a silver gel pen that would show up on the dark paper. As I looked at the journal, appreciating its beauty, I realized that, in everything, God gives us beauty and blessings.

I decided that if I was going to survive this period of bed rest and stay sane, I had to have a strategy. I had to determine in my heart and mind to focus on the blessings in my life as I endured day after day of staring at the same four walls of my bedroom, unable to care for my family. This journal was going to help me do this.

I wrote "Blessings Journal" in a flourish of silver script on the title page and started keeping record of everything throughout my day that I could be thankful for. This included meals that people prepared and brought for my family; a long distance phone plan that made it possible for me to call my mom and my sister everyday (or ten times a day!); the birds singing outside my window (until that got annoying!); my sweet little 3-year-old, who would climb into bed with me each morning so we could read together for hours without anything else vying for my time; my precious children; and the hope of new life growing inside of me; and on and on. As I began to focus on and record the God-given blessings in my life, my task of staying in bed became easier, my attitude changed, and my outlook became brighter!

Why do we take so much for granted? Is it only when we lose something or don't have it that we can learn to appreciate it? Our health, our jobs, home, food, the people in our lives. Having a heart of thankfulness helps us to see the blessings God has given us and to have a brighter outlook each day.

Michelle Stewart

Sweeten Your Life

*Start your own Blessings Journal,
and record all you have to be thankful
for. If that sounds too overwhelming,
just write a few things on the page
here to get you started!*

Chocolate Mousse

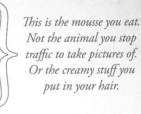

This is the mousse you eat.
Not the animal you stop
traffic to take pictures of.
Or the creamy stuff you
put in your hair.

Ingredients:

1 cup cold whipping cream

½ cup powdered sugar

¼ cup cocoa

1 teaspoon vanilla

Directions:

Beat everything until mixture is stiff. Spoon into small bowls or pre-made tart shells. Eat immediately!

Top Ten at 2 A.M.

I'm in that wonderful aging phase in a woman's life I call "reverse puberty." Consequently, hormonal bloodstream levels in our house are often beyond legal limits for safety of operation. Also, as a result, I have acquired my own personal weather patterns. High and low pressure systems can move in at any time with Death Valley heat or Antarctic cold.

Early this morning, around 2:30, I suddenly awoke from a state of restful bliss to searing temperatures and useless racing mental activity. I felt like I had downed a shot of Starbucks triple espresso—straight, no cream.

To cope with this, I did the truly spiritual thing and got up and played FreeCell on my computer. I lost a lot—actually I cheated at losing by quitting before I did. (Does anyone else do that?) Anyway, my choice of coping activities wasn't working, so I went back to bed and tried to be spiritual and pray. I've heard multiple people say not to pray in bed because you will fall asleep. Don't believe them. My mind just raced more, thinking about all the things people needed prayer for. I was wider awake than ever.

To amuse myself I started to think up a top ten list of survival tips for stumbling through this phase of my life. For those of you who are there with me—tape this list to your portable fan! For those of you not there yet, save it, you will need it someday! For those of you who have already exited gracefully, send me *your* top ten list!

Be prepared! Carry bulky sweaters and T-shirts for quick phone booth changes.

Always carry sunglasses. Great for hiding those droopy sleep-deprived eyes or teary red and puffy ones.

Avoid sad movies. Or have a pillow handy, and be prepared to stuff your sobbing face into it in the middle of the movie theater.

Don't say what you're really thinking. Your thoughts are no longer your own. One minute you love them, the next you love them not. Just say mmmm… and you will keep your mouth out of jail.

Buy stock in Kleenex. You'll buy so much of it, you might as well try and make a few bucks.

Avoid "relationship talks." You might as well admit you don't know who you are right now, so there's no point trying to figure out what's wrong with your relationships. You'll only confuse yourself (and them) more.

Don't watch makeover shows. Whenever you're tempted, repeat to yourself, "Reality TV isn't real, reality TV isn't real, reality TV isn't real." Then get your best smile and sense of humor out of the closet and put them on. You'll look maaaaaavalous!

Forget about sleeping. Think of it as an opportunity for that "alone time" you've been craving.

Do the right things. Our moms have been trying to tell us this all our lives…eat your vegetables, get some exercise, and for heaven's sake, *take care of yourself!*

Go for the gold. There's a crown waiting for you at the end of this race. Persevere. Live and breathe the life of the Holy Spirit. Trust God. Spend as much time with him as you can. You're being refined as gold, pure gold. You know you want that bling, so go for it!

Linda Crawford

Sweeten Your Life

No matter what season of life you're in, find a reason to smile. Thank God for giving you a sense of humor—and be sure you tell at least one joke today!

Frothy Cappuccino

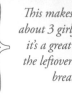

This makes enough for about 3 girlfriends. And it's a great way to use the leftover coffee from breakfast!

Ingredients:

⅔ cup chocolate syrup

2 cups cold coffee

2 cups vanilla ice cream
(use low-fat or frozen vanilla
yogurt for healthier option)

Ice

Directions:

Put the chocolate and coffee into a blender and quickly mix. Then add the ice cream and blend until smooth. Pour over ice and enjoy right away! If you're in a fancy mood, you can add a swirl of whipped cream on top.

God Loves Girlfriends

Get together with one, two, or even more of your girlfriends, and celebrate your friendship. Here's stuff to do together:

- Take time to share which of the devotions you read in the past few weeks was most meaningful to you, and why. It's OK if you all are at different places in the book—just share what God is putting on your heart.

- Share an area of your life where you need your friends to be praying for you. And listen to the needs of your friends so you can pray for them. Remember to keep these confidential. Write each person's name and one word beside it to prompt you in prayer for her this week.

_____

_____

_____

_____

_____

_____

_____

- Go for a walk. If the weather's great, go outdoors. If it's not so great, head to a mall, the gym, your church, a school, or anyplace where you can walk and talk indoors. Enjoy sharing life together!

Yesterday's Garbage

> *No, dear brothers and sisters, I have not achieved it, but I focus on this one thing: Forgetting the past and looking forward to what lies ahead.*
> (Philippians 3:13)

I received a message through my e-mail that someone I used to know from school wanted to be my "friend" on Facebook. The only recollection I have of this girl was that she called me a bad name on the playground in fourth grade. That's the only thing I can remember about her! Did we ever talk to one another in junior high or high school? I may forget what happened yesterday, but I can tell you down to the last detail what happened on that playground over 35 years ago!

Do you ever have trouble letting go of something from your past? A grudge perhaps? Maybe it's past sins (either yours or someone else's) that you think you just can't let go of. Holding on to the garbage of yesterday will never help you move forward in your life. It's a waste of time to keep going back there!

Paul, who wrote Philippians, explains it so well when he tells us to forget the past and look forward to what lies ahead. You can never look forward in your life if you're constantly looking backward. Looking back doesn't make you stronger, and it won't heal you.

Don't buy into the lie that forgiving yourself or others makes you weak. On the contrary, only those who experience Christ's grace and mercy can be strong enough to forgive! When you allow the God, who forgave you of all your sins, to work and move in your heart to let go of the past, it will be the most freeing experience you can ever imagine.

And if you're wondering what happened with my "friend" from the past, I finally decided to add her to my list of Facebook friends—but then couldn't find her request. (The truth is, I'm not that "Facebook savvy.") But maybe she'll find me in the future!

Debbie Stevens

Sweeten Your Life

When you take out the garbage today, say a prayer for someone you're holding a grudge against. As you toss the trash, ask God to help you toss those feelings of resentment and embrace his love and grace instead.

May the words of my mouth and the meditation of my heart be pleasing to you, O Lord, my rock and my redeemer.
(Psalm 19:14)

Pleasing to You

"What is wrong with you!?"

OK, this wasn't really me *asking* my son a question, I was clearly yelling at him! And as tears immediately filled his eyes, I wished I hadn't yelled. I'd asked him repeatedly to pick up his room, and now I was frustrated that he'd chosen not to do this task. Instead, he'd been distracted by the imaginary world of young boys. I didn't want to hurt this little boy that I loved so much, but I did because I let my frustrations control my mouth.

So many times I think that same statement, "What is wrong with you!?" I think it about people who are slow in line, cut me off in traffic, don't follow directions, or just plain irritate me. Inside my head I'm wondering why they can't just do what they should be doing. Why can't they move along efficiently and be courteous to others?

What's wrong with *me*? What kind of Christian example am I setting to those around me? I may not have yelled at strangers, but I'm sure my facial expressions and body language spoke loud and clear. What's wrong with me is that my heart isn't in the right place at times like this. I'm thinking only of myself.

During a recent Bible study, Psalm 19:14 challenged me. My words and my heart could not have been pleasing to God. I needed to be more aware of whether my words and my heart were pleasing to God. Every step I take, every word I think, every deed I do should be pleasing to the Lord.

I apologized to my son. I told him that Mommy shouldn't have yelled at him and said those things to him. I asked him to forgive me. With my arms wrapped around him and a kiss on his cheek, he forgave me. I also asked God to forgive me and help me to be pleasing to him. And in that moment…I believe he was.

Jodie Wilson

Sweeten Your Life

Write Psalm 19:14 on an index card, and put it next to your toothbrush (since that goes in the same mouth that your words come out of!). Every time you brush your teeth this week, read this verse and consider what it means to your life in that moment.

The Bag

I look up to the mountains—does my help come from there? My help comes from the Lord, who made heaven and earth!
(Psalm 121:1-2)

The bag was black with pockets everywhere. It wasn't the most attractive bag I'd ever owned. In fact, it was more functional than anything. But the bag and I had been inseparable for months. Wherever I went, it went with me. It carried documents I needed for the food bank I was running for my church. The bag protected everything I needed to stay organized. And the bag contained my personal items as well: driver's license, lip balm, checkbook. But there were other items in the bag that were more important to me than anything else in it. Items that spurred me to check and double-check to make sure I had the bag with me at all times.

These "other items" were a wide array of medications for stomach ache, diarrhea, migraines, and nausea. I'd been nearly immobilized for a year by sickness before doctors finally diagnosed my illness as a bacterial infection. After two weeks of sulfur-tasting pills, the bacteria was gone, but the fear and habits of being sick for so long remained. Merely contemplating going anywhere would bring an onslaught of the symptoms that had kept me homebound. But with the bag, I felt safe. If things got really bad, at least I would have my medicine to help me feel better.

Internally I struggled. I was better now, wasn't I? Why should I continue to feel this way? As I drove the 17 miles of gravel road that took me to the food bank every week, I begged God for freedom. I longed for a day when I would no longer need the bag. But I would look to my right and see the bag on the passenger seat, an ever-present reminder of my weakness.

GOD SO LOVED THE WORLD...THAT HE CREATED CHOCOLATE

For months the bag and I were close companions. We accomplished much together, taking care of my family and preparing food boxes for needy people. I continued to pray. And I continued to make sure I had the bag.

Then, on the drive home after an exceptionally busy day, I remembered we needed milk. It crossed my mind to call my husband to see if we needed anything else. Keeping my eyes on the road, I reached for the bag next to me to get my cell phone. As my hand grasped air, I glanced over to see if the bag had fallen on the floor. It wasn't there. I pulled over and searched the car. It wasn't there. Slowly returning to my seat, my amazement grew as I realized that I must have left the bag at home. Better still, I hadn't felt incapacitated even once the whole day. My heart swelled with sweet freedom, and I rejoiced that God had answered my prayer!

Do you have a "bag" that you rely on? Ask God to free you from whatever is weighing you down and keeping you from trusting him!

Crystal-Starr Caward

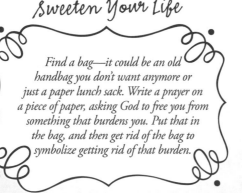

Sweeten Your Life

Find a bag—it could be an old handbag you don't want anymore or just a paper lunch sack. Write a prayer on a piece of paper, asking God to free you from something that burdens you. Put that in the bag, and then get rid of the bag to symbolize getting rid of that burden.

God Cares... Even About Your Undies!

> And why worry about your clothing? Look at the lilies of the field and how they grow. They don't work or make their clothing, yet Solomon in all his glory was not dressed as beautifully as they are. And if God cares so wonderfully for wildflowers that are here today and thrown into the fire tomorrow, he will certainly care for you.
> (Matthew 6:28-30)

I received a package of underwear for Christmas (yes, someone thought that was the perfect gift for me!). As I typically do with new undies, I washed them. Sadly, I discovered too late that they were a bit small. Since I'd washed them already, I knew I couldn't return them. So I wondered, "Who do I know that is just a bit smaller than me that I can give these to—who wouldn't think I'm weird for giving her underwear?!"

I thought of a woman in our church who has four boys and is a bit tight financially. I put the washed, new underwear in a brightly-colored bag and discretely gave it to her the next Sunday at church. To my surprise, she gave me a big thanks and told me she had just asked God in prayer for new underwear because she needed some. Wow! I was not only thankful and in awe that God had brought her to my mind, but also about how this faithful woman had placed this seemingly insignificant need at God's discretion through prayer. By the way, she smiled at me the next time I saw her and said quietly, "They fit!"

Kristin Watson

Sweeten Your Life

What's a tiny need in your life? Or a huge need? Nothing is too big or too small to share with God. While you're getting dressed or putting on your makeup today, mention those needs to God. He's listening!

God Loves Girlfriends

Get together with one, two, or even more of your girlfriends, and celebrate your friendship. Here's stuff to do together:

- Take time to share which of the devotions you read in the past few weeks was most meaningful to you, and why. It's OK if you all are at different places in the book—just share what God is putting on your heart.

- Share an area of your life where you need your friends to be praying for you. And listen to the needs of your friends so you can pray for them. Remember to keep these confidential. Write each person's name and one word beside it to prompt you in prayer for her this week.

_____

_____

_____

_____

_____

_____

_____

- Head to the movies! Or if nothing great is playing, rent a DVD you've all been wanting to watch, pop some popcorn, and have fun viewing a film together. Chick flick? Action film? Or artsy drama? Pick something you'll all enjoy, and then talk about the main themes of the movie afterward. Question for the day: Whom do you want to play you in the movie of your life?

Eating, Exercise, and Laughter

> And even though "I am allowed to do anything," I must not become a slave to anything. You say, "Food was made for the stomach, and the stomach for food." (This is true, though someday God will do away with both of them.)
> (1 Corinthians 6:12-13)

Battling my weight has always been a part of my life. I've never been thin enough to suit myself. I remember someone telling me when I was a young girl that a woman can never be too skinny or too rich. Thus, I used to go without eating all day long, so much so that my dad would take us to the ice cream parlor just to get me to eat something. Of course, I couldn't say no to ice cream! Not exactly great eating habits!

One day a few years after I had had my last baby (still not too skinny or too rich), I was praying while washing dishes. I was asking God to please help me lose weight. As I turned away from the sink, I noticed a plastic bag on the counter. The writing on the bag made me laugh. It said, "Eat less. Exercise more." I had to amend my prayer. I said, "Thank you, dear God, but that's not exactly what I had in mind. I was thinking more along the lines of some nice, easy miracle diet to lose weight."

As I've gotten older, my perspective has changed, and I've become more philosophical. These days I pray, "Thank you, God, that I don't have to worry about my weight. Now I simply have to worry about the health problems I'm facing because I never learned how to eat right. Also, thank you, Lord, that I did start exercising and have continued to do so. And by the way, dear God, just in case there's been a slight oversight, I am still neither too skinny or too rich. However, I am grateful that I won't have to deal with those issues for an eternity!"

Rose Holloway

Sweeten Your Life

While you're having breakfast this week, tell God what makes you laugh. He's interested in every aspect of your life and has a great sense of humor—even when he's teaching you not to become a slave to anything.

The Homecoming

My nephew, Gabriel, has just returned from Afghanistan. He has been gone almost one year. We've been so excited and anxious for him to get home. Gabe's wife, Autum, and their young daughter have been here in the States with the rest of the family, awaiting his return.

We knew the approximate date Gabe would return, but because of security reasons, we weren't told the exact day and time until just a few days before his arrival. When I found out he was back on our safe United States soil, I just broke down. And when we went to his homecoming party, my emotions almost couldn't stay intact when I first saw him. All the months of worries, concern, and continual prayer washed over me with such gratefulness and relief that he was finally home, safe—it all was just too much to contain any longer.

Autum and some of the other wives spent two days decorating and preparing for the long-awaited homecoming. She took extra care to dress herself and 3-year-old Brianna in their Sunday best. They both looked so pretty. Finally, her bridegroom had come home!

Since Gabe's return, I've been pondering how this is so much like the return of our own Bridegroom, our precious Jesus. The Bible gives us many signs of his nearing return, but the Word says no one, not even the Son, knows the day or hour of Christ's return. We are to be ready for his return. Can you imagine the emotion we'll feel when we actually get to see him?!

Autum prepared for Gabe's return. What are you doing to prepare for the return of our King? Is there someone you still need to tell about God's saving grace? Is there something in your life you need to be doing differently? Think about it. I don't want you to miss that homecoming!

Ruth Teal

Sweeten Your Life

Consider what it means to "be ready" for Christ's return. Write your thoughts here.

_____

_____

_____

_____

_____

_____

_____

_____

_____

Measuring Up

Give, and you will receive. Your gift will return to you in full—pressed down, shaken together to make room for more, running over, and poured into your lap. The amount you give will determine the amount you get back.
(Luke 6:38)

Do you ever feel as if you're being "measured"? I do!

There are some days when it seems as though "not enough" is the theme. On these days I feel as though I will never measure up! To what? That depends on the day! Some of those days I believe I'll never be the woman I know God created me to be. On other days I think I'll never be the mother my kids deserve, or I can't measure up because the laundry's not done or there's no milk in the fridge. It seems as if there's a small voice whispering in my ear, reminding me that no matter how hard I try, it will never be enough. On those days, I just want to throw in the towel and say, "See! No matter how hard I try, it's never enough! I give up!"

Then there are days when "too much" is exactly how I feel. These are the days when I laugh at an inappropriate time or offer a critique to someone who truly needs encouragement. Times when I am just plain loud, talking over someone needing a listening ear, or I'm demanding something from someone who has no way to deliver. I don't use past tense because I still do these things! And once again, that voice in my ear reminds me that I am too loud, too inconsiderate, and too demanding. On those days, I want to say, "I quit! I'll just go live in the woods so I don't have to interact with people! I will never get it right!"

There are also days when I'm right where I am supposed to be. I have the patience needed to be kind to a frustrated cashier. My friend calls and I stop what I am doing and give her my full attention. A friend enters my mind; I call and hear the gratitude in her voice as she tells me how frustrated she's been. I pray with a co-worker who's struggling. I take a moment to think of others in the world who are suffering and pray for them.

How do I get to those days where I'm right on target? On those days, I know I've taken the time to connect with God in the morning, and to remind myself that this day is not about me. These are the days I try to give to others in whatever way possible. And on those days, my measuring cup is full with the perfect measure of God's love, and I am grateful to pour it out for all around me.

Brenda Christiansen

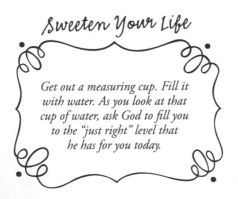

Sweeten Your Life

Get out a measuring cup. Fill it with water. As you look at that cup of water, ask God to fill you to the "just right" level that he has for you today.

True Confessions From Underneath a Basket

> You are the light of the world—like a city on a hilltop that cannot be hidden. No one lights a lamp and then puts it under a basket. Instead, a lamp is placed on a stand, where it gives light to everyone in the house. In the same way, let your good deeds shine out for all to see, so that everyone will praise your heavenly Father.
> (Matthew 5:14-16)

I know many women who are content with living under the radar. They're well-intentioned, hard-working, and God-loving women who know how to get things done. They are the ultimate selfless multitaskers who make everything look easy. Launching a new product at work? Easy. Planning a church potluck dinner for 50? No problem. Maintaining the family calendar with four sporting events, three music lessons, and two doctor's appointments in just one week? A cakewalk. But being a company *spokesperson* for that new product? Unthinkable. *Leading* the church retreat that happens before the potluck dinner? A frightening thought.

I must now confess that I am one of these women.

I don't enjoy the spotlight. I deplore my own birthday parties and feel very awkward with any public attention. I realize that there's a difference between self bragging and being a light for others, but I struggle to find that intersection. So I hide my light under a basket.

I'm in good company. There are many quiet leaders here

underneath the basket. The good news is that the Bible says our deeds speak just as loudly and spread as much light as our words. But there are times I wonder if I'm limiting my effectiveness in building God's kingdom here on earth. I think about Rosa Parks, who shocked the world (and probably herself) by refusing to go to the back of the bus that day. That was a basket-raising moment for sure. I think about Clare Boothe Luce, who, after an unconventional and often traumatic first half of life, became an accomplished writer and politician. Or Mother Teresa, who let her actions speak loudly but didn't shy away from opportunities to share her convictions in speeches.

Let's commit to getting out from under the basket when we see opportunities to inspire others or bring about change. We may need our sunglasses the first few times but we'll get more comfortable with the light as we shine for Jesus!

Connie Dean

Sweeten Your Life

What about you? Do you let your light shine in quiet ways or in public ways? How might God be challenging you to get out from under the basket and shine more brightly for him? Write your thoughts on the next page.

GOD SO LOVED THE WORLD…THAT HE CREATED CHOCOLATE

Over the Moon

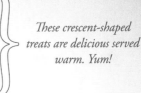

These crescent-shaped treats are delicious served warm. Yum!

Ingredients:

½ cup chocolate chips—milk, semisweet, or dark

¼ cup coconut

2 tablespoons chopped nuts (any kind you like)

1 can (8 oz.) of refrigerated crescent dinner rolls

Directions:

Mix the chocolate, coconut, and nuts together. Separate the dough into 8 triangles. Put about 1 tablespoon of the chocolate mixture on each triangle, making sure you use all of the mixture equally on the triangles. Gently press the mixture into the dough. Roll up each triangle so the narrowest end is on the outside. Place on an ungreased cookie sheet; curve each roll a little to create a half-moon shape.

Bake at 375 degrees for 10-12 minutes or until lightly brown. Let cool just a few minutes (so you don't burn your mouth!) and then enjoy.

God Loves Girlfriends

Get together with one, two, or even more of your girlfriends, and celebrate your friendship. Here's stuff to do together:

- Take time to share which of the devotions you read in the past few weeks was most meaningful to you, and why. It's OK if you all are at different places in the book—just share what God is putting on your heart.

- Share an area of your life where you need your friends to be praying for you. And listen to the needs of your friends so you can pray for them. Remember to keep these confidential. Write each person's name and one word beside it to prompt you in prayer for each friend this week.

_____

_____

_____

_____

_____

_____

_____

_____

- Have you ever heard the phrase "You've been punked!"? This describes a situation when someone has had a practical joke played on him or her. Instead of "punking" someone, "pink" them! With your girlfriends, decide on another friend who needs encouragement. Head to a dollar store, and get a bunch of pink things, like lotion, a coffee mug, pens and paper, and so on. Tuck them into a pink bag with a note that says, "You've been pinked!" Add a few words of encouragement. Then leave the pink bag on her doorstep. You'll have fun doing this—and you'll make a lasting impression on a friend!

Come Away

He lets me rest in green meadows; he leads me beside peaceful streams. He renews my strength. He guides me along right paths, bringing honor to his name.
(Psalm 23:2-3)

Recently when going through a particularly stressful situation in our family, I sensed the Lord drawing me to come away with him. I felt that he was instructing me to stop at a parking area beside the lake on my way home from work each day. He wasn't calling me to prayer. I was simply to be still and to quiet myself before God.

Each time I would sit in my car and watch the water. Sometimes it would lap gently. Other times the wind would whip the top of the water into whitecaps. The sea gulls would ride the small waves or soar just above the water. Gazing at God's amazing creation was extremely calming.

Most of the time I could only stay for five to ten minutes. Even in that small amount of time I was amazed at how my anxieties gently rolled away as I watched the water lapping against the banks of the lake.

In these quite times, God began to speak to me about how much I had allowed fear and anxiety to overtake me. The weight of the situation felt crushing. Some days I felt that I would surely explode with the pressure. But when I sat still in the presence of the Lord, he restored my soul, renewed my strength, bolstered my faith, and filled my heart with his indescribable peace. I began to realize that although I had been praying, "I trust you, Lord," my fear and anxiety over the circumstances spoke much louder of the fact that I didn't trust him completely. God is amazing and can do in a moment of stillness what we cannot accomplish with all our struggle and worry.

Shirlene VanWinkle

Sweeten Your Life

Come away with the Lord, and sit quietly in his presence for a few moments today. Simply sit and gaze upon God's beautiful creation. Maybe it is not a lake, but a tree in your backyard or the beautiful blue sky and fluffy white clouds. Don't speak— simply listen for God's voice.

*The Lord rescues the godly; he is
their fortress in times of trouble.
The Lord helps them, rescuing them
from the wicked. He saves them,
and they find shelter in him.*
(Psalm 37:39-40)

Not a Nightmare

I grew up in a perfect world. My family was close knit and active in church. My siblings and I obeyed our parents (most of the time!). Our mom and dad loved each other, and *divorce* was a word that was foreign to us. I lived a dream life!

Then I grew up, and that dream was suddenly taken from me. I saw my mom and dad taken by death, experienced the heartbreak of seeing my sister and daughter go through divorces, discovered I had cancer, and had my heart broken when my precious grandson went through a period of rebellion.

I wanted to wake up from this nightmare and return to my dream life! But this is the reality of the world we live in, and no one is exempt.

Did you dream of how your life would be, only to have your dream crushed by reality? It may have been a dream of a happy marriage that ended in divorce. The dream of a long life together became the untimely death of a loved one. The dream of perfect children or grandchildren, but instead they go astray. No matter what it may have been, it was devastating and shook your world and maybe even your faith.

What do you do with unbearable heartache? Do you bury your face in a pillow and live a life of hopeless defeat? It's all in what kind of choice you make.

I've cried many tears, but I've made a choice to ask for God's help and to trust his unfailing love. I choose to hold on to the promises that God gives us. He has never failed me, why should I doubt his care for me now? Psalm 37:39-40 assures me there is hope and protection in God. I just have to trust and believe it!

Sammye Barnard

Sweeten Your Life

Rest your head on your pillow for a few moments, and tell God about your dreams, and about those dreams that haven't turned out as you planned. Then write a note to God, telling him you're placing your trust in him instead of in your dreams. Tuck that into your pillowcase tonight as a gentle reminder to truly put things into God's hands.

The Best China

Children are a gift from the Lord.
(Psalm 127:3)

When I was just a young girl, my first set of dishes for my hope chest was a set of Melmac. That's a high-class name for plastic! However, I was very proud of the dishes until my parents blessed me with a lovely set of china.

Now I love beautiful dishes of china, pottery, and stoneware and would probably have a vast variety of every type and pattern if my cupboards would permit. Through the years I have compiled a large collection of the very old and popular pattern called Old Country Roses, and I am always adding to my set, along with a set of chintz china.

When a dear woman from our church passed away a few years ago, she left a wonderful old set of Desert Rose dishes for me, knowing that I would appreciate them as much as she did. I treasure them not only for the beauty of the dishes themselves, but also for the precious memories they offer me of my friend. Just looking at them reminds me of the times that she served me tea or coffee in one of the lovely cups and of the many hours we shared together.

One thing I've noticed about women who have special china is that they tend to save their best dishes and only use them for special occasions. These lovely dishes are only brought out for holidays or birthdays, so they're seldom used. I decided a long time ago that I wouldn't do that. Instead, I resolved to use them often, even if it was just for an ordinary dinner. I want my own family to feel that they're special enough to me to merit using my very best dishes.

It's true that these special dishes are more fragile and must be handled with care; however, even though the dish may break, it can be replaced. Your family cannot be replaced. My little granddaughter has her very own tiny Old Country Roses teacup. If she breaks it, we'll simply look for another. She knows that she is special to Nana, and we love to sit together with our matching teacups to share a cup of tea. When we share tea, we are creating a treasured memory.

Remember that your family and friends are more valuable than anything you own. Make sure they know how special they are!

Wanda Fielder

Sweeten Your Life

Bring out your best china or finest linens, and set a gorgeous table. Let your family or a few friends know you value them and recognize them as gifts from God.

Adjusting to God's Plan

Take delight in the Lord, and he will give you your heart's desires.
(Psalm 37:4)

When my daughter, Tonya, finished her master's degree and was job hunting, I prayed that God would provide her with a job that was nearby. Specifically, I prayed she'd find a job that was only a day's drive away from our family home in southern Illinois.

Well, God gave Tonya a position teaching at a college in Maryland. I wasn't mad at God, but I was very disappointed. I managed to see Tonya about every three months, flying to see her at times or meeting her at other locations such as family vacations taken together. But I still longed for that closeness of a day's drive.

Then, due to some changes in my life, I gave up my little VW "bug." My husband, Gene, and I bought a bigger, more comfortable car. We thought it would be great for traveling and decided to take a road trip to see Tonya. We left on a Thursday afternoon and got to her house Friday afternoon, just after she got home from teaching.

Our family was together every minute and had a blast until Sunday morning, when Gene and I left at 7:30. We stopped a few times to eat and to take breaks. And then, we were about two hours from home, this thought struck me: God did answer my prayer! *It was only a day's drive!* It only took me two years and two months to figure this out! All this time, in my head, "a day's drive" meant nothing over eight hours. It all came down to my definition of a day. God's day and mine were different, but my prayer had been answered.

The moral to the story? As we are praying about our heart's desires to the Lord, let God figure out the answer! Be open to adjust to *his* plan!

Ruth Teal

Sweeten Your Life

Just for fun, get out a road map for your part of the country (or look one up online), and see where you can drive in a day. Is there any place you could go to that you've never been before? Consider taking a weekend trip to a new destination simply to see what new adventure God might have in store for you. And if you can't get away, at least drive home a different way one day this week. Ask God to open your eyes to new sights, sounds, and experiences he has in store for you!

God Loves Girlfriends

Get together with one, two, or even more of your girlfriends, and celebrate your friendship. Here's stuff to do together:

- Take time to share which of the devotions you read in the past few weeks was most meaningful to you, and why. It's OK if you all are at different places in the book—just share what God is putting on your heart.

- Share an area of your life where you need your friends to be praying for you. And listen to the needs of your friends so you can pray for them. Remember to keep these confidential. Write each person's name and one word beside it to prompt you in prayer for each friend this week.

- Bake a treat! Gather in one of your kitchens, page through this book, and find a recipe you all want to try, and make it together. And…eat it together, too! Enjoy the sweetness of the dessert as you enjoy the sweetness of your friendship. You might take a plate or dish of whatever you've made to a girlfriend who couldn't join you just to remind her you love her!

Methuselah Goes to College

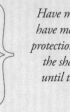

Have mercy on me, O God, have mercy! I look to you for protection. I will hide beneath the shadow of your wings until the danger passes by.
(Psalm 57:1)

We own the world's worst dog. His name is Tobe, but my husband calls him "The Tobenator." We adopted him from a Golden Retriever Rescue organization; someone returned him because, we believe, Tobe is mentally challenged.

A couple of weeks ago, we experienced a tragedy in our home. Tobe got into the kid's pet turtles and the end result looked like a massacre. Their little turtle island was chewed up and strewn down the hall from one end of the house to the other. Needless to say, no turtles were found in the bowl. Tobe, with his snout still dripping wet, was yelled at and sent to his kennel. It was not a good day at our house. During clean up we found Miley (my daughter's turtle) down the hall in the corner dazed and confused. But Methuselah (my son's turtle) was nowhere to be found. After several days of mourning, we tried to move on.

Two weeks later my daughter, who is away at college, calls. "Mom! You'll never guess what I found in my dorm room!" She found Methuselah in the middle of her dorm room floor. I screamed with shock and delight! It became clear what must have happened that night. Tobe scooped up Methuselah into his mouth, flung him around, then swatted him like a hockey puck right into my daughter's room, where he must have landed in her clothes, only to be picked up and thrown into the trunk of her car!

Have you ever felt like Methuselah? Life has carried you away, flung you around, and then swatted you like a hockey puck only to leave you stunned to find that you're still alive? Thankfully, we have a God we can cry out to in times of trouble and hide beneath the shadow of his wings until danger has passed!

Debbie Stevens

Sweeten Your Life

If you have a dog, stop to play with it today. If you don't have one, find a friend with one and stop by to say hello. Think about how carefree the life of a dog or cat is, and ask God to help you have the ability to not worry about the things of life but to trust him as our master instead.

Skeet Shooting With Gingerbread

Most new brides have at least one adventure in cooking that becomes the family story told over and over again (usually told by the husband at every family gathering!). Mine began early in my marriage after a conversation my husband and I had about family recipes and favorite memories of holiday treats. As I told him about my grandmother's gingerbread, I could almost smell the spicy fragrance filling our kitchen. In my mind, I could see her at the farmhouse table, ingredients spread out around her big brown mixing bowl as I waited to lick the bowl. The die was cast. I just *had* to have gingerbread!

I dug through my recipes and found the treasured paper with Grandma's recipe. I quickly scanned the list of ingredients and saw that I had everything needed in my cupboard. All seemed normal until I got to the final ingredient. The recipe said "flour to thicken." Wait a minute. Just how much flour does it take to thicken? I decided it should be easy to determine when the batter was thick enough. After all, I had seen Grandma do it many times. I added flour, beat the mixture, and then added more flour. When it was the "perfect" blend, I poured it into the waiting pans and popped them into the oven. The smell I remembered began to fill my home.

However, a strange thing happened. The cakes didn't rise! I checked my ingredients. Yep, I had put all the right things in to make it rise, but it just sat there baking. When the timer went off, I pulled the pans out, thinking, "Oh well, it doesn't look very good, but I'm sure it will taste just fine." Wrong again! The cakes were as hard as rocks.

Trying to make light of the situation, my husband said, "Don't worry, I can use them as clay targets!" What could I do but join him in laughter?! After 32 years of marriage, the mention of gingerbread reminds us of clay targets, Grandma's recipe, and the value of finding humor in life's "mistakes."

Molly Lewis

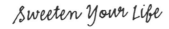

Sweeten Your Life

Do you have a funny story that started out as a frustrating moment? Write it down on the next page and begin to share it. The next time you feel yourself becoming upset because something's gone wrong, stop and ask yourself, "Can I find humor in this?" When you do, you will find that laughter truly is the best medicine!

God So Loved the World…That He Created Chocolate

Chocolate Pie for Cheaters

This pie is so easy it's like you're cheating as a cook!

Ingredients:

1 large chocolate bar (4.25 oz.)
—you can choose milk, dark, or with nuts

1 tub (8 oz.) of whipped topping

1 pre-made graham cracker crust (buy this—don't make it!)

Directions:

Melt the candy bar over low heat, stirring the whole time. Let it cool a few minutes, and then stir it into the whipped topping. Pour this into the graham cracker crust. Refrigerate. Eat. Be happy.

Time Travel

I awaken bleary-eyed to the sound of blasting music. Whoa, 6:00 a.m. comes way too early! I guess the shower will have to finish the job of waking me up. Two pieces of toast will probably become the extent of my breakfast. A wet gloomy day, not to mention the cold, is predicted today. To my chagrin, I notice that my work clothes are also going to need to be ironed. The car needs gas and will there be time to go to the grocery store before or after work? This is just the beginning of my day.

Lunch time could be my quiet time to read or reflect or relax, but that has not happened in quite a while. Instead, there are errands to run either for myself or for my boss. After work I go to a meeting, and then there's a trip to the store before I head home to fix supper. This seems to be happening more and more often. Others tell me of their hectic lives. We all want to find some free time.

Time, time, and more time seems to be a perpetual need. I wonder if anyone has ever considered time travel as a helpful solution for a lack of hours in the day. And what about God? When do I plan time with him in my day and have a peaceful moment with the Lord?

Psalm 31:15-16 reminds me that the future is up to God. I don't need time travel, I just need to slow down and take time to be with God. I'm thankful for the rest and peace that comes when I do put my life in God's hands and let him take care of the rest!

Melinda Lange

Sweeten Your Life

Tape a tiny piece of paper over the face of your watch for a day. Every time you look at your watch, let the piece of paper remind you that your time actually belongs to God. And each time you see the paper, thank God for his love and for caring about the hours and minutes of your life.

I Can't Remember!

When the car pulled to a stop a few yards ahead of me as I walked, I assumed someone needed directions. Our small town is designed on confusing angles, and I often get asked for directions to the schools or parks while I'm out walking.

As soon as I approached the passenger's window, the woman driving exclaimed, "Hello, stranger!" I drew a blank. She looked familiar. She sounded familiar. My mind raced. Who was she and how did she know me? She asked me how I'd been. I answered vaguely. She told me she'd recently had another baby and was making a quick trip to the Dairy Queen for a birthday cake. I listened for clues to help me remember who she was, but my mind grasped nothing.

She pulled away, and I continued to walk, still grasping for identification. Blocks later, a brief image flashed into my mind, and it all came rushing back. I had visited her home after she'd attended our church several times. She had a baby, and I'd treated her to ice cream on one of the first days her husband returned to work. She hadn't returned to church, and after a couple of notes and calls, I'd lost touch.

That was a couple of years ago. She now lives in the same town where I live, different from the town where I attend church and where she used to live. Our paths crossed again, and I was sure God had a purpose. Now that I knew her name, I made a mental note to call the church soon to track down her phone number.

I had a lunch date the following day, and as I walked in the door, I glanced across to the opposite entrance, where the same woman was entering with her two children! She exclaimed, "Twice in two days!" I didn't want to take attention away from the friend I was meeting, but I asked if we could get together soon and exchanged phone numbers. I'm not sure why God re-collided our lives, but I'll soon find out. I've learned God never squanders a connection he orchestrates.

Susan Lawrence

Sweeten Your Life

Has someone popped into your mind today? Pick up the phone and reconnect. Or perhaps God will cross your path with someone who needs your encouragement today (or someone who will encourage you!). Be attentive to the people around you, and enjoy God's connections.

God Loves Girlfriends

Get together with one, two, or even more of your girlfriends, and celebrate your friendship. Here's stuff to do together:

- Take time to share which of the devotions you read in the past few weeks was most meaningful to you, and why. It's OK if you all are at different places in the book—just share what God is putting on your heart.

- Share an area of your life where you need your friends to be praying for you. And listen to the needs of your friends so you can pray for them. Remember to keep these confidential. Write each person's name and one word beside it to prompt you in prayer for each friend this week.

_____

_____

_____

_____

_____

_____

_____

- Find a simple service project you and a couple of friends can do together—trim the bushes for an elderly neighbor, paint the bathroom of someone who's recently been bedridden, or babysit for a family with a lot of children. Do the project together, and it will be a ton more fun! Plus you'll be a blessing to someone in need.

Rough Edges, Smooth Finish

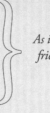

As iron sharpens iron, so a friend sharpens a friend.
(Proverbs 27:17)

One Sunday morning as I entered the choir stand at church, I bumped my leg on a rough corner, and it tore a gaping hole in my stocking. I was so upset that I couldn't even fully engage in the service because I was sure everyone was looking at my stocking! Needless to say, no one saw the hole or even cared. In fact, people complimented me on my lovely ensemble without noticing what I thought was a huge flaw in my appearance.

I'd let that rough piece of wood have such a negative effect on my day. It got me thinking about other rough edges I see around me. For example, a finely crafted sailboat, the intricately designed banister on a steep staircase, or even my favorite park bench. All of these things were once ragged pieces of wood. But in the right hands, each became something else. Something beautiful.

We have our jagged edges, too. And there are rough spots in our lives. In addition, God knows that we can cause deep splinters if anybody bumps us in the wrong place. We need others in our lives who can see the beauty beneath our rough edges and are willing to diligently "sand" until we are smooth to the touch.

God places people in our lives to bring balance and depth. We need to learn to appreciate others' rough edges—and allow them to be sandpaper in our lives, too. So pull out the sandpaper and get to work. Don't complain about the chips in their wood. Find a belt sander and make them shine. There's

GOD SO LOVED THE WORLD...THAT HE CREATED CHOCOLATE

great joy in knowing that my friend will work with me and for me to help shape me into who God wants me to be. True friends understand your roughness, but will not allow you to splinter others without first attempting to smooth it out. And friends won't throw you away just because you are a little rough around the edges.

Yachecia Holston

Sweeten Your Life

Pull out an emery board, and use the sandy surface to neatly smooth the edges of your fingernails. While you're doing it, thank God that you're not as rough as you once were, and thank him for friends who are sanding and polishing your heart to smooth over the remaining rough edges.

Hope and Help From a Sticker Patch

And endurance develops strength of character, and character strengthens our confident hope of salvation. And this hope will not lead to disappointment. For we know how dearly God loves us, because he has given us the Holy Spirit to fill our hearts with his love.

(Romans 5:4-5)

The giant autumnal cottonwood trees provided the perfect backdrop for a royal blue and silver Schwinn woman's bicycle. And on an Indian-summer day in Wichita, Daddy's determination to teach me to ride my twelfth birthday present was 1960's best gift.

Our driveway had a teardrop island in it with the garage ramp at the widest end. At the other end was a white wooden gate—the kind kids stand on and swing. Golden honeysuckle grew along the left fence line, while a wicked patch of goat-head sandburs grew along the right.

I scrambled onto the gleaming black seat as Daddy steadied it from behind. Heavier than he should have been, he was wearing his usual white T-shirt and blue jeans. Bending over was not a sustainable posture for him, so I had barely positioned my feet when he started pushing and yelled, "Pedal through the gates!"

Good advice. Except...

Terror of toppling and disappointing my father transfixed me, riveting my eyes on that sticker patch. Thus, the first crash was inevitable. Eleven crashes later, however, I still had not ridden that bike. Sweat-drenched and out of patience, Daddy finally gave up and disappeared. The basket was mangled, and the horn was destroyed. I was painfully perforated, but I didn't dare quit.

Looking down the driveway for the thirteenth time, my heart sank. My stepmother was inside the house watching the pathetic display, so I knew humiliation awaited me if I couldn't manage even one success. Fortunately, years of Sunday school had taught me to pray. "How do I do this, God? Everybody's watching."

Apparently, God was, too. Like a whispering angel, I heard, "Look only where the pavement starts." I took a deep breath, steadied myself, powered up again, and ordered my eyes to lock on to that blessed, gravel-strewn threshold that suddenly held so much promise 30 feet *beyond* those gates. That's all it took to finally sail past the sticker patch like a champion, one who never fell there again.

Thirty years later, as a stream of freshmen college students filed into their first class with me, I silently remembered all the failures of that birthday. It was my job to inspire academic success, and I hoped my embarrassing milestone could help because every student in that room had flunked out of high school. As a new Christian, I prayed again, "How do we do this, God?" Happily, I recognized the Whisperer's voice. "Unqualified though you were, you counted on me; I am enough; I did the rest." Suddenly I knew God's hands had guided my victory lap and would guide my class.

Marian Victori-Angela Echo

Sweeten Your Life

Are you stuck somewhere because of sticker patches in your life? Ride a bike today, even if you have to borrow a tricycle. When you stand on the pedals, tell God you will stand on his faithfulness today. Repeat daily.

Ice Cream Sandwich Sweetness

This dessert looks fancy, but is ultra easy!

Ingredients:

19-20 ice cream sandwiches
(yes, the kind from the freezer
section at the store)

1 container (8 oz.) whipped topping

1 jar (16 oz.) hot fudge topping

Directions:

Line the bottom of a 9x13 pan with 1 layer of unwrapped ice cream sandwiches. You may need to cut some in half to fit in your pan, based on the size of the sandwiches. Spoon the fudge topping over the layer of sandwiches, and spread it gently. Then spread half of the whipped topping over this. Make a new layer of ice cream sandwiches on top of this, changing the direction of the bars for this layer. Top this with the rest of the whipped topping. If you have any ice cream sandwiches left over, feel free to eat them now.

Cover this and put it in your freezer until you're ready to eat it. Take it out about 15 minutes before serving so it will be easier to cut. The slices look so pretty with all the layers. Only you will know how easy it was!

Staying Shiny

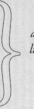
Once again I polished my old skillet to a blemish-free shine. How many years I've been doing this—polishing those copper-bottom pans with every use! They're not even displayed where anyone can observe my diligence. I do it because my mother and dad gave me that set of pans some 35 years ago. Dad said they were the best, and I was delighted to have them. I exclaimed at the time, "I'm going to keep them looking just like that!"

Dad snorted something sounding like "Harrumph!" and with a sarcastic little laugh, "That's what your mother said, and look at hers."

Those many years ago I silently determined, "I'll show you both." Though they're not around to see, I never put one away without polishing and drying it to a brilliant gloss. As I rub vigorously to remove the black stains, I wonder whether Dad ever knew. Can he look down from heaven where he has been for 20 years and see shiny copper? I doubt it. But I still try to please my father.

But my heavenly Father does know. He's not interested in the cleanliness of my cookware. Instead, he's interested in seeing his reflection in my life through my obedience to his will. He must be sad sometimes to observe the areas that I keep polished (that really aren't important to him) and those in which I fail to glow in faithfulness. I often hurry through the day, thinking only of tasks to accomplish and giving little thought to someone in my world who needs to see the light of Christ glow through my encouraging word or helpful act.

Laura Winship

Sweeten Your Life

Pull out a dust cloth or polishing rag. As you dust and clean, ask God to show you any area of your life that needs his special reminder and your willing action to shine forth into your world's darkness.

Another Chance at First Love

First love. Just the thought of him makes you smile and feel so special. You can't wait to spend some time with him. You chuckle when you think of how your friends describe you as "changed" since you've been with him. You always find a way to mention his name in conversations, much to their chagrin. Yet a few of your friends have told you privately that they wish they had what you seem to have with him—not just the fact that he has professed his love to you dozens of times, but how he shows you that love. It really makes them jealous!

Imagine one day you opened his hand and saw that your name was tattooed there. His explanation: He prays for you and thinks about you every time he uses his hands. Wow! Every day you look forward to your talks. He's always there on time and listens even to your wildest ramblings. When he speaks, you want to listen, too, because he always has something wise or funny to say. Oh, you could go on and on about him.

But then…time goes by.

It's been awhile since you had a long talk with him, and it seems as if you're always preoccupied when you do make it to your meeting spot. Lately your conversations have been you rambling on about your day and by the time you finish, it's time to rush to your next appointment. You hate leaving him hanging and always promise to stay longer the next time. So many things happen in between visits now. Sometimes you forget your meeting. You've heard the messages he leaves for you and you hear the sadness in his voice. You did not mean to forget, but you had so much to do—for him and his children. Surely he understands.

He still meets his responsibilities. He is a good man. He tells you about how he feels now that you're not as close as before, but he still does special little things for you.

Your relationship is obviously falling to pieces, and the problem is on your end. Can it be salvaged? Each day presents us with another opportunity to return to the first love we had for Christ. How will you return today?

Natasha Pemberton-Todd

Sweeten Your Life

Remember your first crush? Your first true love? What drew you to that boy or man in the first place? Now think of Jesus. What drew you to him? Write those thoughts on the next page. Think of two things which once brought fulfillment in your relationship with Christ. Choose one you have not done in a while and do it today!

PB & C Bars

Peanut butter and jelly is a favorite flavor. But peanut butter and chocolate is even better! These no-bake bars are simply yummy!

Ingredients:

2 cups peanut butter

¾ cup butter, softened

2 cups powdered sugar

3 cups graham cracker crumbs

2 cups semisweet chocolate chips

Directions:

Beat 1¼ cups of the peanut butter and all of the butter in a bowl until creamy. Beat in 1 cup of the powdered sugar. Then use your hands to work in the other cup of powdered sugar, the graham cracker crumbs, and ½ cup of the chocolate chips. Press this mixture into a lightly greased 9x13 pan.

Melt the remaining ¾ cup of peanut butter and the remaining 1½ cups of chocolate chips over low heat, stirring constantly until the mixture is smooth. Spread this over the graham cracker and peanut butter mixture. Refrigerate for an hour or longer so the chocolate is set. Cut into bars and share with your girlfriends.

God Loves Girlfriends

Get together with one, two, or even more of your girlfriends, and celebrate your friendship. Here's stuff to do together:

- Take time to share which of the devotions you read in the past few weeks was most meaningful to you, and why. It's OK if you all are at different places in the book—just share what God is putting on your heart.

- Share an area of your life where you need your friends to be praying for you. And listen to the needs of your friends so you can pray for them. Remember to keep these confidential. Write each person's name and one word beside it to prompt you in prayer for each friend this week.

_____

_____

_____

_____

_____

_____

_____

_____

- Head out for coffee! Whether it's a latte or cappuccino or you opt for chai tea, take time to savor the flavors of your warm drink as you savor time with your girlfriends. (And think about inviting someone new to come along! It's a nonthreatening way to get acquainted.)

Keep Me Company

Afterward Jesus went up on a mountain and called out the ones he wanted to go with him. And they came to him. Then he appointed twelve of them and called them his apostles. They were to accompany him, and he would send them out to preach.
(Mark 3:13-14)

I recently joked with some friends that I would love to be put on an isolated island to enjoy being by myself for a while! Living with a husband and three teenagers leaves *very* little "alone" time in my home! A few days later, I travelled to Shanghai, China on a business trip. Once I arrived in my hotel room, I felt very alone and was filled with a huge sense of separation. I was literally on the other side of the world from most of my family and friends in Massachusetts! I had gotten my wish for isolation, and it turns out, I didn't like it that much.

In Mark 3 Jesus appointed his 12 disciples. One aspect I find very interesting is the job description, beginning with the words, "to accompany him." Sure, they had other responsibilities, but the first thing listed was companionship! They were there to keep Jesus company.

We were created as social beings, in need of relationships and intended for life together. Being a "get it done, check off the to-do list" type of person, I often put higher value on tasks rather than relationships. After all, relationships take time! But they are so valuable and needed!

Thankfully, the Lord is always with me, and I learned a special lesson during my time in Shanghai. God used this time to teach me to rely on him in a new way, but also to appreciate the closeness of the relationships in my life.

Kristin Watson

Sweeten Your Life

Grab a pen and paper, pick up the phone, or type an e-mail. Thank one of your girlfriends for walking with you in your life and for being close to you just to keep you company!

Overflowing With Joy?

I have told you these things so that you will be filled with my joy. Yes, your joy will overflow!
(John 15:11)

I have decided to rediscover the joy that seems to have taken a slight vacation from my life, and bring it back center stage. This has made me dig into the differences between happiness and joy.

Happiness is 100 percent circumstantial. When everything's coming up roses, the sun is shining, and all your ducks are lining up in a nice little row...that's when you can be happy. But finding joy comes from a much deeper place inside you. Joy comes from knowing that regardless of what is going on around you—the good, bad, or ugly—you can still have peace and rest, secure in knowing that Jesus is still Lord, and he still has everything under control. Especially when everything is beyond your control. This makes me think of a friend from the Bible, Paul.

Paul was not an early follower of Jesus. He was actually on his way to hunt down early Christians for trial and execution. Then Jesus spoke to Paul clearly and suddenly, and Paul was transformed in an amazing way. He became the greatest missionary of all time.

Through his letters to other early Christians, we can see that Paul was joy-filled. But I can't imagine that he was always happy. His circumstances were often less than ideal and, more times than a few, life threatening. In 2 Corinthians 11:24-25 Paul says, "Five different times the Jewish leaders gave me thirty-nine lashes. Three times I was beaten with rods. Once I was stoned. Three times I was shipwrecked. Once I spent a whole night and a day adrift at sea." This passage continues, adding being robbed, experiencing hunger, thirst, cold, and other hardships to Paul's list of experiences.

Now, I don't know about y'all, but I'd be a little hard pressed to remain joy-filled after being beaten, stoned, left for dead, and so on. Yet Paul moved forward with unabashed passion for Christ. No matter the situation, he remained firm in his faith.

When life seems hard to me, I have to remember that it's only through the awesome and almighty power of Christ that we have the strength to do anything. This means my happiness no longer depends on my situation, but instead I reflect the joy I have found through my Savior. My situation has not changed. However, my outlook has done a complete 180!

Dallas Louis

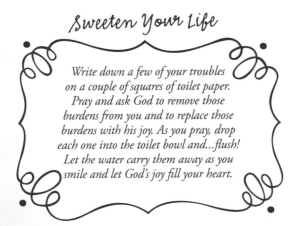

Sweeten Your Life

Write down a few of your troubles on a couple of squares of toilet paper. Pray and ask God to remove those burdens from you and to replace those burdens with his joy. As you pray, drop each one into the toilet bowl and...flush! Let the water carry them away as you smile and let God's joy fill your heart.

A Red-Shoes Day

You will show me the way of life, granting me the joy of your presence and the pleasures of living with you forever.
(Psalm 16:11)

Surely you've heard the expression "red-letter day." Do you know the origin and meaning of the phrase?

The expression "to have a red-letter day" developed in the early 1700s from the long-term practice of using red ink to indicate high days and holidays on church calendars. In a year dominated by black-ink days, these few were boldly proclaimed in bright red as the most special, most memorable, and most joyful days in a Christian's life.

Well I recently had a "red-shoes" day instead of a red-letter day. You see, the shoes in my closet have always been black, brown, or white (with the occasional renegade cream or navy). My shoes are practical and unobtrusive.

Occasionally one of these functional pairs of shoes wears out, and I have to shop for a replacement. So I went looking for a practical black sandal. Then...I saw them. Glaring, audacious, and oh-so-red. I wanted them. But I did the "right thing" and asked the salesclerk to bring me a pair to try on in brown. She came back with a box and said, "We didn't have your size in the brown shoes; the only ones we have in your size are the red shoes." And she proceeded to open the box before me.

Why in the world at 46 years old, would I suddenly have a desire to put on red shoes? So I rationalized. I'll just try them...I put them on and turned hesitantly to the mirror. I couldn't believe those shoes were on my feet! I sheepishly told the salesclerk that I had never *ever* owned a pair of red shoes.

I think the Holy Spirit prompted her to say what she said next…"Well, it's about time you did then!" she exclaimed. She was so right. So *right!* My shoe closet was an indicator of how I had chosen to live my life. Focus on the practical. Be responsible. Act like an adult. Be unobtrusive. *Be a black-, brown-, and white-shoe Christian!*

The Holy Spirit took those red shoes on my feet and used them to unlock a long barricaded room in my heart. I loved them. They delighted me. They made me feel so joyful and free. And I wanted everyone to notice them! I had to share my enthusiasm with the shoe salesclerk before I left the store. She will never know how much God used her to minister to me through that sale.

For the rest of that day, I stuck my feet in everyone's face. "Look at my red shoes! See my red shoes?" I drove my husband and teenage daughter crazy as I kept repeating every few minutes, "I *love* my red shoes!"

Why? I love them so much because they opened my heart to a new level of love for Jesus. Childlike delight in him. And I don't care who sees it. As a matter of fact, I *want* people to see it. Just like I want them to notice my red shoes, I want them to notice the free-flowing liberty in my spirit to express the joy of knowing and loving Christ. No more just black, brown, and boring. My life is meant to be an expression of red-shoe delight in God!

Do you have *your* red shoes yet?

Linda Crawford

Sweeten Your Life

Next time you're shopping, try on something entirely outside of your comfort zone. See if God challenges you to brighten your life in a fresh way!

GOD SO LOVED THE WORLD…THAT HE CREATED CHOCOLATE

Rockin' Rocky Road Bars

This is a way to make your regular brownies into something special.

Ingredients:

1 box of brownie mix and the ingredients to make that mix (probably eggs, oil, and water)

1 cup chocolate chips—milk or semisweet

2 cups miniature marshmallows

1 cup chopped nuts (any kind you like)

Directions:

Make brownies according to instructions on the box. Do not over-bake them. Remove from oven and immediately sprinkle the chocolate chips over the top. Wait about 5 minutes, and then spread the now-melted chips evenly over the surface of the brownies. Sprinkle the marshmallows and the nuts over this, and return the pan to the oven. Bake at 350 degrees for 3-5 minutes—just long enough for the marshmallows to melt a bit.

Cool and serve. (It's easier to cut these if you dip your knife in water first.)

A Christmas Journey

But Mary kept all these things in her heart and thought about them often.
(Luke 2:19)

For me, it takes a moment of quietness on the couch at night—with the TV off, the computer in "sleep" mode, and the last bit of laundry tumbling in the dryer—for my thoughts to surrender to Christmas. My gaze falls on a beautiful, old-world Santa pillow, and a few ceramic Santas of various sizes, shapes, and eras assembled together on a table. Who is Santa? In the quiet, it is a question to ponder.

He is a real part of Christmases past in my life. As a child, I had an overflowing imagination that became reality to me. I was a true believer in Santa Claus! I heard the jingle of reindeer bells in the front yard, Santa always left cookie crumbs on the plate set with anticipation, and he always finished the milk. The carrots had disappeared; a snack for his flying reindeer. The stockings were always filled, and Santa almost always left me at least one thing I had requested in my letter. I loved Christmas morning! I was the poster child for all the perfect Christmas TV ads.

But in third grade, my Christmas world was shattered when a friend matter-of-factly told me there was no Santa Claus. That was the year that "Rudolph the Red-nosed Reindeer" and "Silent Night" became a sorrowful blend of what Christmas meant to me. Santa was simply a spectacular story, and I was growing up.

As Christmases passed, I wondered more about Mary, the teenage mother of Jesus. How could she face an angel who told her that she had found favor with God, that she was going to have a baby, and that she was to name him Jesus? I was amazed that Mary had the courage or the faith to say to the angel, "May everything you have said about me come true."

God's Word, in the book of Luke, has since spoken to me and continues to change my heart as I absorb the account of the blessed baby boy who grew up and gave the greatest gift ever given in the history of time. God came to us in that tiny body and was cradled in the arms of his teen mother. She nursed him, potty-trained him, and delighted at his childish antics. She guided him through his teenage years and let him go when the right time came. Then Mary, 33 years later, mourned for her Son again at his death. Knowing he suffered so greatly, and willingly died *because he loved me*, is almost more than I can imagine!

My third-grade heart, which was shattered by the reality that there is no Santa Claus, now stands in awe of the Christ. My Savior, Jesus, has promised me eternal life simply because *I believe* in him and his glorious resurrection! He is not a story, but the truth of *Christ*mas.

Kathy Samuels

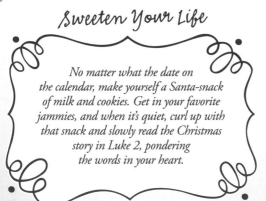

Sweeten Your Life

No matter what the date on the calendar, make yourself a Santa-snack of milk and cookies. Get in your favorite jammies, and when it's quiet, curl up with that snack and slowly read the Christmas story in Luke 2, pondering the words in your heart.

God Loves Girlfriends

Get together with one, two, or even more of your girlfriends, and celebrate your friendship. Here's stuff to do together:

- Take time to share which of the devotions you read in the past few weeks was most meaningful to you, and why. It's OK if you all are at different places in the book—just share what God is putting on your heart.

- Share an area of your life where you need your friends to be praying for you. And listen to the needs of your friends so you can pray for them. Remember to keep these confidential. Write each person's name and one word beside it to prompt you in prayer for each friend this week.

_____

_____

_____

_____

_____

_____

_____

_____

- Find a fun way to sing with your girlfriends. Turn on the radio (turn it up loud!) and sing along. If the time of year is right, go Christmas caroling. Head to a nearby nursing home and sing with the residents. Pull out a guitar, and sing favorite campfire songs from your childhood. Gather around a piano, and sing hymns you love. Whatever way works for you and your friends, take the song in your heart and put in on your lips!

Too Much Clutter!

My daughter and her husband had gone on an overnighter to celebrate their anniversary. I stayed at their home to baby-sit my grandchildren, Lily and Kian. I looked into my granddaughter's room and saw a terrible mess. I told her we were going to clean out this clutter tomorrow. "Where will I put all my stuff?" she asked. I told her I would get her a new shelf for games and puzzles and that brightened up her gloomy look a bit.

It took us all day. We had piles of Barbies, piles of Polly Pockets, piles of various coloring and craft items. Plus stacks of books to be passed on to her little brother. The one pile that wasn't getting very big was the giveaway or throw-away pile. "But I need that," Lily would say. "But do you play with it?" I asked. "Well, sometimes."

We took a lunch break and then got right back to it. Sorting and sweeping. Sorting and dusting. She did manage to part with a few small items to be sent to a mission group our church supports. I started to think we might actually get 'er done.

As we started to put things back into the room, I realized we had some items that didn't belong to any particular category. We found an old cloth carryall she no longer used, and we put all the miscellaneous stuff into it. I hammered a nail to the side wall in her closet and hung it there. She labeled this bag "Stuff." This wasn't trash to her. All of these things meant something. She could not bear to part with them, but they just didn't have a place to belong.

This whole process, the piles, and the "stuff" left over made me think about life. Do you have clutter in your life? I know I do. I've sorted out my problems: finances, relationships, guilt. I got everything organized. There were even some things I decided I could part with. But just like Lily, I had that pile of stuff that had no place to belong.

Now what? Give it all to Jesus. Everything. Even the leftover stuff. He knows what to do with every burden, every situation, even when we don't.

Suzanne Page

Sweeten Your Life

Find something that's clutter in your home or office. Let this represent a burden in your life that you want to get rid of. Hold that item in your hands as you pray and ask God to take this burden, this unwanted stuff, from your life. Then…get rid of that item! Toss it out, and remember that you've "tossed" your problems into the hands of Jesus as well.

Trust in the Lord with all your heart; do not depend on your own understanding. Seek his will in all you do, and he will show you which path to take.

(Proverbs 3:5-6)

As our 4-year-old daughter played in the indoor play yard, she found herself up higher in the enclosed tunnel than she wanted to be. Typically our two older children are there to assist, but they were with their grandparents. This left her without their help and feeling scared.

My husband began to coach our daughter on what she needed to do to get down. Her foot was only a couple of inches away from the next step below her, so he instructed her to simply put her foot down. She began to cry repeatedly saying, "I can't!" He patiently continued to coach her, telling her that she could. He tried desperately to convince her that what he was telling her was true and that all she had to do was trust him.

During this time I was getting aggravated. After all, I could easily climb up and get her, and the whole thing would be over. As I headed in to rescue her, my husband instructed me to just sit down! This went on for probably 10 or 15 minutes, yet it seemed an eternity. Finally, our daughter put her foot down and discovered that she was safe. She realized that she had been afraid of nothing and that the step was directly below her, precisely as her father had said. She merely had to put her fear aside and trust him.

Immediately my thoughts went to our heavenly Father. My husband had been a great example of how God is with us in this situation. He was patient, but didn't rescue our daughter. How many times have we been afraid to take a step that our

Father has told us to take? How many times have we put our trust in our own abilities, rather than what our Father says we can do? How many times have we allowed someone else to rescue us from a situation, rather than wait upon our heavenly Father?

Sherri Kitts

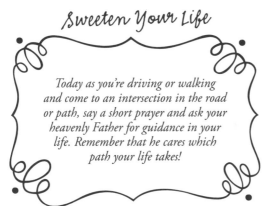

Sweeten Your Life

Today as you're driving or walking and come to an intersection in the road or path, say a short prayer and ask your heavenly Father for guidance in your life. Remember that he cares which path your life takes!

pray About It!

 *Don't worry about anything; instead, pray about everything. Tell God what you need, and thank him for all he has done.*
(Philippians 4:6)

When my daughter was 17 years old, she began talking excitedly about the big day—her eighteenth birthday—when she could move out of our home and be on her own. All of a sudden panic settled on me. I began thinking about all the things she couldn't do for herself. Balance a checkbook, cook her own meals, keep her room clean. I felt such guilt that I had failed to teach her all the survival skills she needed to enter adulthood.

Not that I hadn't *tried* to teach her to cook. Her younger brother still talks about her chocolate chip cookie baking experience when she used cornmeal instead of flour. He ate them anyway and told her they tasted pretty good. Nevertheless, a fear settled on me that she wasn't ready. And it was all my fault.

Fear has a way of sneaking up on us when we aren't expecting it. For a few weeks I drove myself and my daughter crazy trying to use every situation as a teaching moment. Somehow I thought I had to teach her in a few short months everything I had learned in my entire life. Finally, as I prayed about the situation and asked God for wisdom, reason took over, and I realized that when I was 17, I didn't know how to run a household either. Somehow I had survived the transition to adulthood and eventually learned all the things I needed to know. And I knew that my daughter would do the same.

Each new day brings new experiences and new opportunities for fear, guilt, worry, and stress to creep into our lives. Whether it is over children or spouses or friends or jobs or school or any other part of our lives, it is easy to let fear reign in our minds instead of trusting God. But when we remember to pray about the situation first, to tell God what we need, and to thank him for all he has done, then miraculously his wonderful peace helps guard our minds against the fear and worry.

Shirlene VanWinkle

Sweeten Your Life

Remember yourself at 17, whether that was a year ago or decades ago. What have you learned since then? Write about one key lesson here. Then thank God for the ways he guides your steps no matter how old you are.

Truth or Tradition?

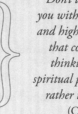

Don't let anyone capture you with empty philosophies and high-sounding nonsense that come from human thinking and from the spiritual powers of this world, rather than from Christ.
(Colossians 2:8)

As pastors of a church, we had the privilege of taking a group of 33 people from our congregation on a tour of the Holy Land. Visiting Israel overwhelmed me on so many levels. It was exciting to experience it and just as exciting to share in everyone else's experiences. The very thought of walking the same ancient stone roads in Jerusalem as Jesus walked was humbling and exhilarating at the same time.

Our thoroughly knowledgeable Jewish guide brought the richness of his ancestry in the Holy Land alive to each person in our group. It was fascinating to watch the rich culture around us. As we visited the Western Wall and saw people of various faiths praying at or catching a glimpse of the wall, we witnessed varying levels of tradition. We saw the orthodox Jewish men with their long side curls and black hats, the women with their heads covered and long skirts, and us, the North American Christians in our tourist garb but respectfully covered.

So many traditions! It made me think about the traditions I follow and whether there is merit in them. My traditions may not be visible to people around me like the orthodox forms of tradition in dress and rituals, but they could be just as restricting. Why do we do the things we do? Does our commitment to our faith come from a real, personal relationship with God or do we follow a set of rules made up by man?

I know I want to be sure that the way I choose to live my life lines up with God's Word and is not dictated by other people or religious standards that don't have true biblical foundation. I remember my mom telling me that when she first came to church as a teenager and asked God to be a part of her life, a woman from that church came up to her and said, "Now that you are born again, you will have to wipe off that red lipstick." It's the miracle of God's love that caused my mom to stay and, thankfully, raise me to know and love the God who accepts us just as we are...and the Holy Spirit who gently teaches us and encourages us in our journey.

I hope I can be an example of that love and keep traditions in perspective. I want to follow the truth, not merely tradition.

Michelle Stewart

Sweeten Your Life

What are the traditions in your life that bring meaning and joy? What are the ones that weigh you down or even take your focus off of God? Write about those on the next page, and consider changes you might want to make. And, if you ever get a chance to visit Israel, take it!

Friendship Fudge

We call this friendship fudge because anyone will be your friend if you give them some of this!

Ingredients:

1½ cups sugar

1 can (5 oz.) evaporated milk

2 tablespoons butter

¼ teaspoon salt

2 cups miniature marshmallows

1½ cups semisweet chocolate chips

½ cup chopped nuts (optional)

1 teaspoon vanilla

Directions:

Mix sugar, evaporated milk, butter, and salt in a pan. Bring to a full boil, stirring constantly. Keep boiling and stirring for 5 minutes. (Set the timer!)

Remove from heat and stir in the marshmallows, chocolate chips, nuts, and vanilla. Continue stirring until the marshmallows have completely melted.

Spread in a greased 8x8 pan. Refrigerate for 2-3 hours or until fudge is firm. Cut into pieces. Eat a few. Share the rest.

If you like minty chocolate, add 2 or 3 York Peppermint Patties into the pan right when you remove it from the heat. Yum!

God Loves Girlfriends

Get together with one, two, or even more of your girlfriends, and celebrate your friendship. Here's stuff to do together:

- Take time to share which of the devotions you read in the past few weeks was most meaningful to you, and why. It's OK if you all are at different places in the book—just share what God is putting on your heart.

- Share an area of your life where you need your friends to be praying for you. And listen to the needs of your friends so you can pray for them. Remember to keep these confidential. Write each person's name and one word beside it to prompt you in prayer for each friend this week.

- Take a walk down memory lane. Pull out your photo albums, and share them with your girlfriends. Even girlfriends who spend a lot of time on scrapbooking rarely show off their photos. And if you're the girlfriend with all your pictures in a shoe box, don't despair! This is about sharing memories, not comparing art skills. As you enjoy photos together, tell the stories that go with the pictures. You'll discover stuff you never knew!

The Keepsake

Be thankful in all circumstances, for this is God's will for you who belong to Christ Jesus.
(1 Thessalonians 5:18)

The glass water pitcher my mom passed down to me had been in her family for years. It was a small, heavy glass pitcher with a large chip on the rim of it. As she presented the pitcher to me, she excitedly shared the story with me of how my great-great-grandmother fell and chipped the pitcher on her way to fetch water from the well when she was a little girl. I accepted this gift from my mom with inadequate gratitude, and placed it on the windowsill of my kitchen where it stayed for years.

At some point I moved the pitcher to the top of the refrigerator. And then one day as I opened the freezer door, the pitcher came toppling down, breaking into a thousand pieces. I screamed in horror as it fell; my heart sank as I gazed upon the glass shattered all over the floor. The wonderful keepsake that had been in my mom's family for so many years, in one swift moment, was now a mess on the floor. How careless I had been! Why didn't I take better care of this precious gift my mom had given me? I felt so ashamed that she had entrusted me with the pitcher—rather than cherish it, I had taken it for granted and ruined it.

As I reflected on this incident in the days following, I was reminded of all the wonderful blessings in my life. I began to question myself. How many times have I failed to show the Lord the gratitude he deserves for all the gifts he's given me? For family, for friends? How am I being careless with the incredible blessings in my life God has entrusted me with? I stopped in that moment and asked God to forgive me and to help me to never again take my many blessings for granted.

Sherri Kitts

Sweeten Your Life

Do you have a keepsake of some kind that has been passed down to you? Use that as a reminder to thank God for the things he's passed into your life. Every time you see it, take a moment to express your gratitude to God. And if you don't have a keepsake like this, choose another special item you cherish to be this same kind of reminder.

Holding My Hand

Another birthday etched its way into my life. I was blessed to have our adult children, grandchildren, and even my parents there with me. My husband took it upon himself to invite them all for pizza and birthday cake. He also surprised me with a watercolor painting done by our friend, artist Rich Marks. He had asked Rich to paint the hand of Christ reaching down and holding on to the wrist of one of his beloved. It's an amazing and beautiful piece of art! My husband had it matted and framed with the word "Security" engraved on a piece of brass and mounted on the frame.

Another gift I received the same day was from our youngest grandson, Jacob, who is eight. On a piece of lined notebook paper, he had drawn a picture of himself and me walking together in front of a very big, bright sun with a dozen flying M-shaped birds in the air. We are holding hands, and we both have big grins including teeth! There are labels written above our heads: "grandma" and "me."

The first painting is hanging prominently on the wall in our entryway. The second is taped to the mirror in my bedroom. Both are precious to me. Now that a few days have passed and I've had time to reflect on both gifts, I sense a deeper meaning from each.

The beautiful painting depicting the hand of Christ conveys a message of how wide and long and high and deep God's love for me is. He holds on to me and lifts me up when I mess up.

I'm safe and secure in his hand for all eternity. It portrays the tender strength of God's comfort, grace, and forgiveness.

The sweet child-drawn picture fills my heart with love for my grandson because I have proof of his love for me. Not only do I receive his hugs and kisses, but I get a picture drawn by him that is just for me! Does Christ feel my love for him, as I have felt Jacob's love? Do I have a picture for my Lord and Savior drawn in my childish hand? A picture of the two of us walking hand in hand through a meadow of wildflowers on a sunny day with big smiles on our faces? A drawing that depicts my desire to spend time with the Lord that I love? God knows my love for him, but it must delight his heart when I tenderly offer a gift given from my heart.

Kathy Samuels

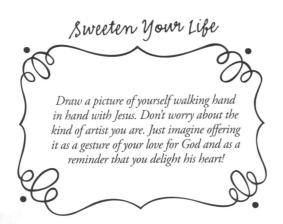

Sweeten Your Life

Draw a picture of yourself walking hand in hand with Jesus. Don't worry about the kind of artist you are. Just imagine offering it as a gesture of your love for God and as a reminder that you delight his heart!

Daddy

For everything comes from him and exists by his power and is intended for his glory. All glory to him forever! Amen.
(Romans 11:36)

I'm afraid my dad is developing Alzheimer's disease. He is slowly forgetting family members' names. But all too soon, I'm afraid, he will forget faces. Sometimes when I look into his eyes, there's a look of hollowness, confusion, and despair. I hate this disease; it's a thief and a robber that's slowly taking my dad away from his family.

Whenever I can't understand the realities of life such as this, I cling to what I do know. I know God says he has a purpose for every one of his children. A purpose that is for good and not evil (Jeremiah 29:11), a purpose for his glory (Romans 11:36). So what possible purpose could God have in my daddy losing his memory and all his physical abilities?

Maybe the purpose is actually for us.

Maybe it is to teach us patience and self-sacrifice. To teach us to be servants like Jesus. Could it be so that we may grow more Christ-like and ultimately...glorify God? If this is true, then my dad is doing a huge part in shaping the face of humility in my family. He is redefining dignity and teaching my mother patience like nothing else could.

Through his handicaps, we are seeking God in a way that maybe we would not have otherwise.

Debbie Stevens

Sweeten Your Life

In John 17:4 Jesus says,
"I brought glory to you here on earth by
completing the work you gave me to do."

What has God given you to do? How do
your actions glorify God, even when
it's hard and humbling? Write
your thoughts here.

Great Is God's Faithfulness

Great is his faithfulness; his mercies begin afresh each morning.
(Lamentations 3:23)

I've had an old hymn rolling around in my head recently. Anyone familiar with "Great Is Thy Faithfulness"? Apparently I'm not too familiar with it because I only know the chorus, which speaks of the unfailing faithfulness of God. He is always there. He is there when we cannot see, feel, or even sense him.

This hymn is based on a passage from Lamentations. I really like Lamentations, which, if you think about it, is sort of morbid. The whole book is filled with the crying, weeping, and wailing over the destruction of Jerusalem. It's a short book, only five chapters, but right smack dab in the middle of this extreme sadness, is a ray of sunshine...a beacon of hope.

> *The thought of my suffering and homelessness is bitter beyond words. I will never forget this awful time, as I grieve over my loss. Yet I still dare to hope when I remember this: The faithful love of the Lord never ends! His mercies never cease. Great is his faithfulness; his mercies begin afresh each morning*
> (Lamentations 3:19-23)

I well remember my "awful times" as well. I remember who I was way back in the day. Those days before the Holy Spirit successfully managed to get my attention. The dark days of even darker choices. Yet this I can call to my mind: As I visit those memories, I can see the hand of God working to protect and shield me. I can see how God guided me. I can (now) see how, in God's perfect timing, I was woken up to the destructive path I was on. I went kicking and screaming because I liked my old life and tried desperately to cling to it. But through the sheer persistence of God Almighty, he showed me this new life was better. I can boldly say I am not who I was.

What about you? Do you need a new life? God's mercies begin afresh each day. Perhaps it's time to start that new day!

Dallas Louis

Sweeten Your Life

Use a hymnal or go online, and find the lyrics to "Great Is Thy Faithfulness." Sing it, hum it, think on it. Be reminded today of God's faithfulness to you, day after day after day.

God Loves Girlfriends

Get together with one, two, or even more of your girlfriends, and celebrate your friendship. Here's stuff to do together:

- Take time to share which of the devotions you read in the past few weeks was most meaningful to you, and why. It's OK if you all are at different places in the book—just share what God is putting on your heart.

- Share an area of your life where you need your friends to be praying for you. And listen to the needs of your friends so you can pray for them. Remember to keep these confidential. Write each person's name and one word beside it to prompt you in prayer for each friend this week.

_____

_____

_____

_____

_____

_____

_____

- When was the last time you played miniature golf? Grab a neon-colored ball, a battered club, and a few girlfriends. Hit the local mini-golf course, and have a great time laughing as you play. Make up funny ways to hit the ball (with your left hand if you're right handed, with your head hanging upside-down…you get the idea!). You don't even have to keep score. Just have fun together.

My Crazy Quilt Life

> *Christ is the visible image of the invisible God. He existed before anything was created and is supreme over all creation, for through him God created everything in the heavenly realms and on earth.*
>
> (Colossians 1:15-16)

The dictionary defines a crazy quilt as a patchwork quilt with no regular design. Well, that certainly rings true in describing my life. Daily routines are difficult as I rush from one commitment to another. Due to a busy work travel schedule, my hours are highly variable as I try to fit in everything important to me: my faith, family, friends, and even my hobbies. On good days, it all works somehow. On other days, one role dominates at the expense of the others. I often wonder how to keep it all together and prevent myself from truly going crazy!

One of my hobbies is quilting and sewing. This pastime keeps me sane. It's my quiet time to immerse myself in creation. I especially like crazy quilts because they're a practical way to use up scraps and are easy to work on over long periods of time.

The crazy quilt's many different sizes and shapes of fabrics represent all the important relationships and roles in my life. There's no such thing as too many pieces. Even the smallest piece is needed to make the quilt whole. Add more color and texture, and the results are even richer. Place unexpected trims and embellishments on top for extra pizzazz, and it gets better yet. You can't overdo it, and it's never really done.

I often wonder if crazy quilts aren't so crazy after all. They always end as a big surprise as a beautiful creation emerges out of the chaos. What's seemingly unplanned by me turns into a stunning and unique work of art. I often wonder if our Creator feels the same way about us.

Connie Deant

Sweeten Your Life

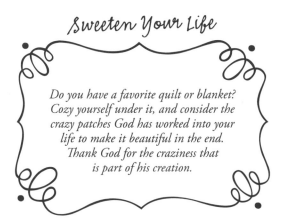

Do you have a favorite quilt or blanket? Cozy yourself under it, and consider the crazy patches God has worked into your life to make it beautiful in the end. Thank God for the craziness that is part of his creation.

Linda's Yums

How sweet your words taste to me; they are sweeter than honey.
(Psalm 119:103)

I was married barely a year, living in a new town for my husband's new job, and didn't know a soul. I landed a job as counter help in a rental shop. Linda worked there, and she soon started inviting me to do things with her.

Linda always had an activity planned. One time we made bread. I'd made quick breads before, but this was "real" bread that actually used yeast! Linda had a recipe book of nothing but breads. We made white, wheat, and rye bread, and braided a strand of each together before baking. Of course, Linda sent fresh-baked bread home with me to enjoy with my husband. But she also gave me the recipe book! Next to each recipe she had tried and really liked, she'd handwritten "Yum!" with a smiley face so I'd know that was a good recipe.

Linda scheduled a "girls' night out" with me about every other month. Once we made jam. Another time Linda shared her piecrust recipe, which makes five crusts that you can store in the freezer for use later. Of course we made pies, and one went home with me… along with the pie recipe book marked with Linda's "yums."

Linda guided me through crocheting, raising a vegetable garden, and crafts, including stained-glass artwork. One winter we spent several evenings in the back of the rental shop where Linda showed me the ins and outs of cutting glass and soldering the pieces together. She let me help with a stained-glass fish…and you can guess what she gave me for Christmas that year.

One summer Linda asked me if I'd like to do a Bible study— just her and me. I'd never done a Bible study before. I said yes. Linda found a small book about women in the Bible, and we would sit outside the rental shop in the sunshine while working through the lessons—my first taste of stories in the Bible. Linda invited me to church, and I started going with her. Eventually my husband came, too.

I lived in that town eight years before my husband's job took us to a new town. I'm now not far from my thirtieth wedding anniversary. I still have the stained-glass fish and the bread and pie recipe books with Linda's "yums" and smiley faces. And I still get a letter from Linda at least once a year—the handwritten kind. She still grows a vegetable garden, she's still in a women's Bible study, and she still finds crafts to do, like turning store-bought cookies into Santas with her grand-niece and grand-nephew. Her latest letter says her biggest joy is the artwork: She creates stage setups for her church's Vacation Bible school.

Linda made time in her busy schedule and spent the time with me. She created in me a sweet hunger to know the God of the Bible, his Word, and the Lord Jesus Christ, and then she fed that hunger. This girlfriend's unlimited friendship has impacted my life for all eternity.

Dianne Butts

Sweeten Your Life

Think of one friend who might need to connect with someone like you. Think of one thing you like to do. Call her and make a date to do that one thing together this week.

Threads of Love

There is no greater love than to lay down one's life for one's friends.
(John 15:13)

My friend was busy on a sewing project, and when I asked what she was sewing, she replied "threads of love." That struck a chord with me, and I began to think of several "threads of love" projects. I'd just recently made a pillowcase for my granddaughter's tiny pillow. I loved stitching it for her and seeing her excitement that it was being made especially for her. Another dear friend of mine spent many hours sewing a beautiful dedication dress for her first granddaughter. Much love was inserted with each hand stitch of lace and trim, and it soon became a treasured heirloom. I also couldn't help but remember as a little girl how many threads of love that my own mother sewed for me. She made sure that I had new attire for special occasions by using her talent in sewing for me.

In the Bible we also see several stories of threads of love. One particular story of renown is the tale of Joseph and his coat of many colors as described in Genesis 37. Because he was such a beloved son, a beautiful coat was made for him by his father. Unfortunately, what was meant to be threads of love actually became a source of hatred toward Joseph from his brothers.

In the book of Acts, we can read about a woman named Tabitha, or Dorcas. She was described as full of good works. She had sewn many threads of love for others in need. When she died, they brought the coats and garments she'd made for them as an expression of the love they felt for her.

God So Loved the World…That He Created Chocolate

Of all the threads of love you can account for, there is none as significant as those our Lord has woven into the tapestry of our life. Much love and sacrifice has gone into every fold of the fabric and every tiny stitch. The hours of agony and pain that he endured to weave a better life for us cannot be forgotten or dismissed. He didn't just contribute a small portion, but he gave his all, the supreme sacrifice. In John 15:13 Jesus declares, "There is no greater love than to lay down one's life for one's friends." What an awesome display of "threads of love!"

Wanda Fielder

Sweeten Your Life

What can you offer your friends and special ones as your threads of love? One idea is the gift of time. Spending an afternoon with an elderly grandparent, taking a child to the playground, or volunteering in your community will weave another thread in the tapestry of your life and in the life of someone else. Every thread, no matter how small, adds to the beauty of the tapestry.

He Owes Me Not

> For the wages of sin is death, but the free gift of God is eternal life through Christ Jesus our Lord.
> (Romans 6:23)

When I was attending college at CSU, Sacramento, I was president of Students for Life. We were going to participate in an event in which our organization would be highlighted, and we would be videotaped for posterity. I decided that I needed a new outfit for the event (a cute pair of shorts and a matching softball button-up jersey, both sporting our school logo), and so I asked God for the money. I only needed about $40—with $40 I could go right down to the Hornet Bookstore and buy them.

I happened to mention to God that he basically *owed* me a new outfit as I was representing him at this event. My conversation with God went on as I stepped onto an elevator. The doors closed, and the elevator promptly got stuck! At that moment God impressed upon me, "I don't owe you anything."

I was all alone, and you can imagine the sheer terror I felt. Had I inadvertently upset God? Several unpleasant scenarios raced through my mind. (Obviously, none came true, as I am well and writing this for you to read!)

I promptly pushed the alarm and within 15 minutes I was rescued. Someone came by, heard the alarm, realized I was stuck in the elevator, pried the doors open, and pulled me out. Today I can actually laugh at my reaction, as I am sure God did.

Thinking back about my desperate desire to get out of that elevator is comical; but, on the more somber side, that experience put into perspective for me my wants, my needs, and just exactly

GOD SO LOVED THE WORLD…THAT HE CREATED CHOCOLATE

what I truly deserve. Since that day, I have never forgotten the fact that God doesn't owe me anything. Everything he has done for me is due to his grace and love. I deserve punishment for my sins, but God has chosen to extend grace to me instead.

By the way, I did get that outfit!

Rose Holloway

Sweeten Your Life

Take time to reflect on what God has given you that you don't deserve. What gifts, relationships, opportunities, and so on has God put into your life that you know are because of his grace extended to you? Write your thoughts here.

God Loves Girlfriends

Get together with one, two, or even more of your girlfriends, and celebrate your friendship. Here's stuff to do together:

- Take time to share which of the devotions you read in the past few weeks was most meaningful to you, and why. It's OK if you all are at different places in the book—just share what God is putting on your heart.

- Share an area of your life where you need your friends to be praying for you. And listen to the needs of your friends so you can pray for them. Remember to keep these confidential. Write each person's name and one word beside it to prompt you in prayer for each friend this week.

- Many of us live in the same location for years but never take in the local culture. Get together with your girlfriends, and visit the local museum, art gallery, or other attraction. Perhaps there's a tea factory in your town or the world's largest collection of antique washing machines! No matter whether it's high culture or…not-so-high, have fun exploring your town together!

Into-Me-You-See

God would surely have known it, for he knows the secrets of every heart.
(Psalm 44:21)

I recently heard intimacy defined as "into-me-you-see." I thought this was a clever definition. After all, isn't that what we all truly desire? Intimacy with those we share our lives with? We want them to see into our lives, and know us well.

Yet as I began to contemplate this catchy definition, I started to wonder if a saying like that can do more damage than good. Do we sometimes have an unrealistic expectation that intimacy should mean into-me-you-see, and then resent it when that someone we thought knew us the best, gets it wrong? After all, how well can we really know someone?

My doubts reminded me of an event a few years ago, my thirtieth birthday, when my husband, who probably knows me better than anyone, proudly handed me a card that included a gift certificate for a day of pampering at a local resort. My husband always gives very thoughtful gifts and since this was a big birthday I knew he must have given the gift extra consideration. At first I tried to be enthusiastic and appreciative...but within minutes I was in tears.

"You really don't know me at all!" I cried. "I would never go to one of those places...I mean, look at these pictures on the brochure! Young men are rubbing half-clothed women—I could never do that! I can't believe you didn't know that about me!"

I was heartbroken that he didn't know me well enough to realize that I'm way too shy to do something like that—especially all by myself. The truth is, as much as we think we may know someone or they may know us, in reality that person will never know our every thought or understand everything inside our hearts. At best, the type of intimacy we can find with another is only second-rate compared to the kind that we can experience with the Lord. By God's design, others will never know us the way the Lord knows us.

Instead of wanting someone to know you intimately, resolve to grow closer to the God who already knows everything about you. Only then will you find true *into-me-You-see!*

Kim Corder

Sweeten Your Life

Even though we can't see into the hearts of others the way God does, we can still pay attention to the likes, dislikes, and special interests of our friends. Start a secret list of things your friends like or of their hobbies. Then surprise them now and then with their favorite flavor of cake, favorite flowers, favorite doughnuts, and so on. They'll be touched to know you cared enough to pay attention. And be sure to thank God for paying attention to every detail of your life!

My Electric Blanket

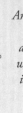

And I will ask the Father, and he will give you another Advocate, who will never leave you. He is the Holy Spirit, who leads into all truth.
(John 14:16-17)

O h! I had a hard time getting out of bed this morning! My bed was so warm and cozy. I live in Houston, and it typically doesn't get very cold down here, but lately the weather has been arctic! We've had snow twice this winter! The temps dipped down past freezing enough times to turn all of my palm trees into Popsicles. Big, brown ugly Popsicles, at that!

So this brings me to my electric blanket, which I'm huddled under a lot this winter. I think my electric blanket was one of the best things I've purchased in a while, except for the fact that on mornings like this, I don't want to venture out of bed! What does the blanket do? It keeps me warm. But I found out not long after I bought it that an electric blanket needs to be covered by a comforter in order to reach its full potential. The blanket has the ability to keep me warm, but it can't do it by itself. It needs some help keeping the warmth tucked close to me.

In the Bible, we read a lot about Jesus' disciples. These men were with him for three years, learning from him, talking to him, seeing firsthand what Jesus was all about. Jesus was investing in them over time so they would be able to continue the ministry of Jesus when he was no longer on the earth. And despite those three years, they often still missed the point. (I sometimes call them the "duh-ciples" because they just didn't get it!)

Jesus knew they were going to need some help once he left the earth. In fact, he knew we were all going to need some help! So Jesus promised the Holy Spirit to continue working in us and to continue his work. You see, the duh-ciples had the ability to preach and spread the good news. Jesus placed that ability within them. But they couldn't do it on their own. They needed a "covering" or Comforter to insulate them so they could fully process everything they had seen, heard, and learned while at the feet and side of Jesus.

Some translations use the word *Advocate*, *Encourager*, or *Counselor* in John 14. But I like the versions that use *Comforter* here. I like the image of my cozy comforter keeping the warmth inside, helping my electric blanket do its job better. And I'm thankful for *The* Comforter, who helps me stay close to God and to follow his plans. Cozy!

Dallas Louis

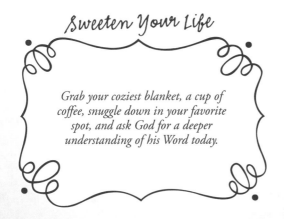

Sweeten Your Life

Grab your coziest blanket, a cup of coffee, snuggle down in your favorite spot, and ask God for a deeper understanding of his Word today.

Bikers, Black Leather, and Church

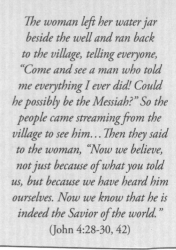

The woman left her water jar beside the well and ran back to the village, telling everyone, "Come and see a man who told me everything I ever did! Could he possibly be the Messiah?" So the people came streaming from the village to see him…Then they said to the woman, "Now we believe, not just because of what you told us, but because we have heard him ourselves. Now we know that he is indeed the Savior of the world."
(John 4:28-30, 42)

One June Sunday after church I stared at the menu in a local fast-food place, vaguely aware of another couple in the restaurant doing the same thing. When I glanced over, I realized they were Debi's parents, a girlfriend I'd known since third grade but had lost touch with over the two decades since school. After a bit of catching up, I asked about Debi.

"Well," her mother offered, "she just bought herself a motorcycle."

"Cool!" I said. "My husband and I both ride, too!" Her mother looked dismayed that I didn't share her disapproval but promised to give Debi my phone number.

In July my phone rang, and I was delighted to hear Debi's voice. We filled each other in on the highlights of our lives (and the makes and models of our motorcycles), and then she asked, "Can we get together?"

"Well, Hal and I have become Christians," I told her, "and we've been invited to ride our motorcycles to visit a church this Sunday. Would you like to ride your bike out and meet us?" I didn't know where Debi stood spiritually, so I felt a twinge of anxiousness. I'd changed a lot since Debi knew me. I wondered what she would think of me and my faith in Christ. Would she think me and my invitation to church weird?

To my total surprise and delight, Debi immediately and eagerly answered, *"Yes!"*

That Sunday Hal and I met her in the church parking lot. We attended church in our blue jeans and leather jackets and then rode to a nearby restaurant for lunch. In August we had some Christian bikers to our house for a barbecue. Debi rode the two-hour trip solo to join us.

In September Debi and I went to a Christian women's conference, and she began going to a church near her home. In October she joined a new members' class and would call me with questions she had about Jesus. Her questions made it clear Debi had made that transition of becoming a believer in Christ.

In November she said, "I'm getting baptized. Can you come?" Since then Debi has faced rough roads, but I've tried to ride some of them with her and mentor her. In a way, Debi reminds me of the woman Jesus met at the well in Samaria: to other women in town, she may have appeared to be the least likely woman to respond to Jesus.

We don't know a lot about the woman at the well, but it's likely she was ostracized by other groups of women in town. She didn't fit in with the usual girlfriends. In today's terms, maybe she smelled of cigarette smoke or rode a motorcycle! But when she met Jesus, she rushed back to town to share the news with *everyone*. Not just her friends! She invited *all* her neighbors to come and meet Jesus for themselves.

Dianne Butts

Sweeten Your Life

Who is the woman you think is least likely to want to know Jesus? Find a common interest and extend an invitation to church or a gathering of women. Just be friends. Let the Lord do the rest.

Mocha Mix

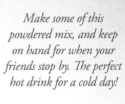

Make some of this powdered mix, and keep on hand for when your friends stop by. The perfect hot drink for a cold day!

Ingredients:

1 cup powdered nondairy creamer

½ cup instant cocoa drink mix

⅓ cup sugar

¼ cup dry instant coffee

Directions:

Mix everything together. Store in an airtight container. To make a cup of mocha, add 3 tablespoons mix to 1 cup boiling water. Add a sprinkle of cinnamon or nutmeg on top if you like.

Healing Begins With "C"

Confess your sins to each other and pray for each other so that you may be healed. The earnest prayer of a righteous person has great power and produces wonderful results.
(James 5:16)

Recently I fell into conversation with two women with whom I was somewhat acquainted. I'd only known them for about two months, and even though I saw them every day, said hello, and sometimes inquired about their well-being, I'd never spoken in-depth with them about personal matters.

This week we "happened" to sit in the same area and eventually fell into conversation. At first we shared our feelings regarding our work, its impact on our stress levels, and how time for self-care almost never happens. We laughed at ourselves and our common foibles. (You know that kind of conversation where one person ventures to share a minor fault and everyone chimes in with "me too!")

Eventually the conversation veered toward family life and personal struggles—both past and present. They started asking for advice on matters concerning their children, knowing that I have a lot of professional experience in the matters they had questions on; nevertheless, the conversation emerged to mutual sharing about some of the previously unrevealed struggles of our pasts. As the conversation went deeper, each of us at some interval observed aloud that "it feels so good to just talk about this."

These ladies had heavy hearts about their children, past mistakes, and moving on. I had my own issues of lost opportunities that still plague me. Yet in the midst of sharing about the struggles, we shared nuggets of hope. At the end of it all, each of us remarked that we wanted to do this every week.

I left there *sad* that our time had to end; *privileged* to have been allowed so deeply into the lives of these otherwise private women; *grateful* for the time we had in the midst of an otherwise humdrum day; and *eager* for the next time we would meet. As I churned the events in my mind thereafter, I couldn't help thinking about how powerful and healing time in a small gathering of women can be. Just the act of confessing (acknowledging) a fault or weakness creates the atmosphere for healing.

When we, with wisdom, expose our faults or struggles, we signal our minds and bodies to begin the healing process. Wow! It's no wonder why Satan seeks to keep us so busy or so riddled with fear that we avoid or miss out on these precious opportunities to gather in small groups to build relationships that go deeper than the perfunctory, "Hi! How are you?" Yet the *healing* we seek is wrapped up in our obedience to his command to *confess*.

Natasha Pemberton-Todd

Sweeten Your Life

What issue comes to your mind as a candidate for the confession list? Write your thoughts here, and then pray about who you might open up to and share with.

_____

_____

_____

_____

_____

_____

_____

_____

_____

_____

_____

_____

_____

_____

Chocolate Cookie Coffeecake

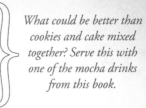

What could be better than cookies and cake mixed together? Serve this with one of the mocha drinks from this book.

Ingredients:

24 chocolate sandwich cookies, chopped (but not crushed to crumbs)

⅓ cup flour

¼ cup butter, melted

⅓ cup semisweet chocolate chips

1 box yellow pound cake mix

¾ cup water

2 eggs

1 cup powdered sugar

4 tablespoons milk

Directions:

Mix the cookies, flour, butter, and chocolate chips in a bowl, and set aside.

Make the cake mix as directed on the box, using the water and eggs. Pour half of the batter into a greased 9-inch or 10-inch tube pan. Sprinkle 2 cups of the cookie mix over the batter. Cover this with the rest of the batter, and then top with the remaining cookie mixture. Gently press down on the cookie mixture that is on the top to make sure it's firmly in the batter.

Bake 50 minutes at 350 degrees or until toothpick comes out clean. Cool about 15 minutes and then turn upside down and remove the cake from the pan. Cool.

Mix the powdered sugar and milk, and drizzle over the top of the cake. Let stand until this glaze is firm. Cut. Eat. Enjoy everyone oohing and aahing over your amazing baking skills.

God Loves Girlfriends

Get together with one, two, or even more of your friends, and celebrate your friendship. Here's stuff to do together:

- Take time to share which of the devotions you read in the past few weeks was most meaningful to you, and why. It's OK if you all are at different places in the book—just share what God is putting on your heart.

- Share an area of your life where you need your friends to be praying for you. And listen to the needs of your friends so you can pray for them. Remember to keep these confidential. Write each person's name and one word beside it to prompt you in prayer for each friend this week.

_____

_____

_____

_____

_____

_____

_____

- A while back we suggested you look at photo albums with friends and share memories. Now's the time to *make* memories! Grab a camera and your friends and take pictures of yourselves in as many funny locations as you can think of. Make prints or e-mail them to each other.

In God's Eyes

She is clothed with strength and dignity, and she laughs without fear of the future. When she speaks, her words are wise, and she gives instructions with kindness.
(Proverbs 31:25-26)

I have always struggled with my looks. You know the questions: Am I ugly, am I too fat, am I not skinny enough, and, oh my goodness, is that hair on my chin? Can you relate?

I have heard so many people say, "God sees you as beautiful" or "God doesn't make ugly." Others assured me, "You're beautiful!" Sometimes I believed it, and sometimes I did not believe it. Then one day I was looking in the mirror, studying each line of my face, looking at my curves of my body. I didn't like what I saw. I saw someone ugly and weak, not strong. Sadly I saw myself as unfeminine.

An ugly voice told me I couldn't change the way I looked or how I felt. "You are too ugly! Who would want you?" the voice rang out. I cried just listening to that evil voice.

However, God, in his power, shut that voice out of my mind. Instead of listening to that voice, God showed me who I truly was. How I looked to him, my heavenly Father. I closed my eyes and saw a vision of myself through the eyes of God. In God's eyes, I saw a different woman; I saw myself beautiful inside and outside. I saw myself soft and feminine. Through God's eyes, I saw dignity. I saw strength.

It didn't matter that I thought I wasn't perfect, or skinny. He saw me as beautiful. I am not abandoned, but loved—totally and completely. God sees me and says, "Wow!" In God's eyes, I am stop-traffic gorgeous.

In his Word, God says to me, "You are a woman. You are clothed in strength and dignity. You are full of life, full of laughter. You are so beautiful."

After carefully thinking and reviewing that beautiful vision, I declared in that moment that I *am* woman. God made me so beautiful and molded me into the woman I am. With this knowledge, I gained strength. I shouted, "I am a woman! World get ready for me!" I moved from seeing myself in my own eyes to seeing myself in God's eyes. What a difference his point of view makes!

Crystal Nicole Livingston

Sweeten Your Life

Use the space here to write five things that make you a unique woman. Then thank God for making you unique.

Rubber Boots

> *The paths of the Lord are true and right, and righteous people live by walking in them. But in those paths sinners stumble and fall.*
> (Hosea 14:9)

The other day I went over to Addisyn and Blake's house to play with them. (They're my grandchildren!) It had been raining but had also been warming up quite a bit from the winter winds. We had all been stuck inside for so long, and I thought it would be so great to be able to go outside and play. But the mud and water were everywhere.

Then I remembered that last fall we gave both of the children old-fashioned rubber boots for their birthdays (which are only 10 days apart). And guess what? I had a pair from long ago, too! I can't tell you how excited they were to see I had boots like them, and we were going out to play! We went out and stomped in every puddle we could find and had a ton of fun. Instead of letting the wet land ruin our fun, we adapted. We had just as much fun, if not more, as we would have had with dry land all around.

God is often this way with us. We can find ourselves praying about problems and situations, asking for help. We're really expecting God to answer the requests in the way *we* want them answered. But his ways are not our ways, and his way of thinking is not like ours (thank goodness!). God might have a plan that involves us outside in the wet and muddy ground stomping around in boots instead of a neat and tidy experience.

We need to place our requests before God. Period. Not tell him how to answer. He has our best at heart, and many times he answers in a way that is much better, a way that we didn't even think of.

Ruth Teal

Sweeten Your Life

Do you have any boots? Put them on, and go look for a puddle to stomp in! (You might need to make a puddle with a garden hose!) Ask God to help you see his paths for you and to give you the ability to walk, run, even stomp along those paths instead of the paths you had planned for yourself.

Signs of the Times

> I am the Lord your God, who teaches you what is good for you and leads you along the paths you should follow. Oh, that you had listened to my commands! Then you would have had peace flowing like a gentle river and righteousness rolling over you like waves in the sea.
> (Isaiah 48:17-18)

While driving through Italy with my family, we decided to take the roads less traveled and do our own exploring. We had left the legendary city of Venice when a heavy fog descended over the land. It was quite creepy as large boat masts began to appear on both sides of the road. Were we still on a road on dry land, or were we on a bridge to some strange place? Very few cars traveled the same road. Every 40 to 50 kilometers we would see signs that we were heading in the general direction of Florence and Rome.

As we neared Florence, we entered some really rough, craggy, mountainous terrain. On fence posts and on trees that were a little distance from the road, signs and posters began to appear. They were just a bit too far away to make out what was written on them. Our curiosity aroused, my husband pulled over, and I hopped from the car to run over to read what one of them said. That done, my feet flew, quickly followed by my body of course, to the car and relative safety once it's doors were locked.

"Just drive!" I told my husband as I laughed and caught my breath. Then I shared what the signs said. "Beware! You are in bandit country! Do not leave your car!"

We joked that the bandits were placing the signs there to lure others out of their cars when they couldn't read them. While this provided a good laugh for our family, it does remind me that God gives us a path to travel in life and guides us along that path. We need to pay attention and follow the signs that God places around us so we can stay on the path instead of leaving it and heading into paths of danger. Keep your eyes open for those signs. They might be in the most unexpected places!

Melinda Lange

Sweeten Your Life

What's a funny travel story from your life? Share it with a few friends next time you get together with them. See how God has used the humorous events of those journeys to brighten your life or teach you surprising lessons!

Making a Difference

> *Pure and genuine religion in the sight of God the Father means caring for orphans and widows in their distress and refusing to let the world corrupt you.*
> (James 1:27)

It is hot and humid, and we are surrounded by soldiers in army fatigues. They were armed and very serious. We have just travelled for 13 hours over bumpy, winding narrow roads into what looks and feels like a jungle to me...but what do I know? I'm from Canada.

I'm a homemaker with a husband, five children, a nice home, and a comfortable life. Twenty-four hours ago, I was taking off my down-filled parka and dodging snowflakes in sub-zero temperatures to check in at the Calgary airport. Now I am wiping perspiration from my face and being asked to follow a female soldier behind a curtain in a makeshift cubicle for security reasons. I obey as I eye the AK-47 slung over the soldier's shoulder. I stand there as she pats me down thoroughly from top to bottom and am amazed at how sweet and gracious these Liberation Tigers of Tamil Eelam are in spite of their violent reputation.

We are in Sri Lanka a mere three weeks after the tsunami disaster with a team of counselors, doctors, and nurses. We have gained access to the north of the country that is controlled by the LTTE. We sleep in bug-infested cots in an abandoned orphanage in Killinochi and are grateful to have some shelter as so many in this area have nothing.

Each day at 5 a.m., the rooster persistently crows to make sure we are all awake. Our morning consists of ice-cold showers, protein bars, and hot tea. We travel two hours each morning to the various refugee camps around Mullaittivu, setting up clinics, and offering assistance and care to the victims. The children are gorgeous. Full of joy and hope! They are so happy to see us and thrilled with the candy and small toys we give them. The camps are in old schools and buildings or simply constructed with wood and tarps.

The day we are at the tarp camp, it pours rain, and everything becomes rivers of mud. The grief and pain are evident in our patients' eyes and though many of them complain of an ailment, we know they are just craving for someone to care. So we listen, we hug, we prescribe when needed, and pray that we have helped them somehow.

The end of our day means another two-hour trek back to our hotel. We stop occasionally to pass through army checkpoints or to buy a warm soda at a roadside stand. We don't stop for bathroom breaks for fear of the most poisonous snakes in the world and, oh yeah, landmines!

We take pictures of boats perched one mile inland and of the piles of ashes and bones. The country is beautifully lush, betraying the vicious force that wreaked havoc, destroying the lives of its occupants and wiping it clean. We stand on a pristine, barren, resort-quality beach and cannot comprehend that this was once a thriving and populated village. I reach down and pick up a lone flip-flop and know that the child that wore it is gone. My mind revolts at the incomprehensible tragedy, but I know I have to face it and dwell on it, to be able to help these people with sincerity.

I travel home from this adventure changed forever because of this trip of a lifetime, thankful for the very small difference I have made in these people's lives and the very huge difference they have made in mine.

Michelle Stewart

Be open to new experiences, no matter how far out of your comfort zone they take you! Sponsor a child through an organization that helps change lives and communities. Pray for children in your community who are in the foster care system. You can make a difference!

Chocolate Bread Pudding

A great way to use leftover bread!

Ingredients:

2 oz. unsweetened chocolate (2 squares)

3 cups milk

4 cups bread cubes

¾ cup granulated sugar

¼ teaspoon salt

3 eggs, well beaten

Directions:

Put the chocolate and milk in a saucepan and heat over low heat, stirring, until chocolate is melted. Remove from the heat and add the bread, sugar, and salt. Slowly stir this mixture into the beaten eggs. Pour the mixture into greased individual custard cups or ramekins.

Set the ramekins in a pan with about ½ inch of hot water. Bake at 350° for about 40 to 45 minutes, or until a knife inserted in center comes out clean.

This is extra delicious served with whipped cream!

God Loves Girlfriends

Get together with one, two, or even more of your girlfriends, and celebrate your friendship. Here's stuff to do together:

- Take time to share which of the devotions you read in the past few weeks was most meaningful to you, and why. It's OK if you all are at different places in the book—just share what God is putting on your heart.

- Share an area of your life where you need your friends to be praying for you. And listen to the needs of your friends so you can pray for them. Remember to keep these confidential. Write each person's name and one word beside it to prompt you in prayer for each friend this week.

- Where's the closest zoo? You may have been with children in the past years, but this time go with your girlfriends. You'll have a whole new appreciation for the creatures God created. Laugh at the monkeys, marvel at the tigers, pet the goats, and try not to feed the animals. Enjoy the beauty and diversity of God's creation!

Broken Shells

How precious are your thoughts about me, O God. They cannot be numbered! I can't even count them; they outnumber the grains of sand!
(Psalm 139:17-18)

I enjoy searching the beach for shells. I'll walk miles of shoreline to find a variety of shapes and colors. Some have been washed onto the beach. Some tumble in and out with the waves, and I grasp for them as they float by. Some poke from the sand, calling to be uncovered.

It seems I find different types of shells at each beach I visit. There's often a type of shell commonly found in an area, and it excites me at first. As I find more and more, I begin to pass by similar shells without pausing. I might find a shell with remarkable coloring or size, but upon further examination, I realize it's broken or otherwise marred with imperfections. I toss it aside. Perhaps someone else will want it.

I'm thankful God doesn't treat people the way I treat shells. God never tosses aside someone who is broken, blemished, or rejected. He tenderly picks up each shell with care. He not only accepts the brokenness, but he knows what caused each rough edge. He knows where the shell started, where its many pieces are, and where all the pieces will end up. No shell is carelessly tossed over his shoulder.

What I pick up on the beach will differ from what someone else picks up. Beauty is in the eye of the beholder. I'm thankful God sees beauty in a drastically different way than people. He's always hopeful, and his eyes see each of us as beautifully made.

Susan Lawrence

GOD SO LOVED THE WORLD…THAT HE CREATED CHOCOLATE

Sweeten Your Life

Cup your hands together, and imagine them full of sand. (Or, if you live near a beach or a playground, go out and fill your cupped hands with sand!) God's thoughts for you cannot be numbered. Imagine counting the grains of sand your hands would hold. Thank God for his limitless passion for you.

Wonderfully Complex!

> *Thank you for making me so wonderfully complex! Your workmanship is marvelous—how well I know it.*
> (Psalm 139:14)

Do we truly believe it when we read that we are both wonderfully complex and marvelous? As women we are often tomboy mixed with girly-girl streaks, trusting yet savvy, gazelle-delicate but lioness-strong, determined yet flexible. We love to express but long to listen; hate to be ignored but hate to be smothered. We look for nuances in conversation, hidden messages in glances. We rock the baby, feed the cat, supervise homework, fix chocolate milk, all the while humming along to the song on the radio.

Wonderfully complex!

On the flip side, we get weary of the tyranny of hormonal fluctuations, emotions that show up when we can least afford them, and the stresses of physical limitations. Why is it we have potential for major emotional upset and instability every 28 days for most of our lives, as well as at major milestones in our lives: pregnancy, postpartum, and menopause in all its various phases?

There are times I want to yell out, "Why did you make me so *horribly* complex? This workmanship is unfair and unkind!"

Then I am reminded: My skin is softer so I can feel the velvet skin of my baby; my heart is delicate so I can have empathy for my girlfriend, a stranger, my husband; my resolve is tougher so I can help others stand firm; my emotions flexible so I can stretch my love deeper and wider. I can multitask so I can accomplish more. I have hormones so I can enjoy pleasure and corral pain.

Sure, I sometimes have to pay attention to not unleashing the self-centered diva in me. I must remind myself not to make life-altering decisions when estrogen and progesterone play teetertotter in my body. But the Bible, in 2 Peter 1:3 tells me, "By his divine power, God has given us everything we need for living a godly life. We have received all of this by coming to know him, the one who called us to himself by means of his marvelous glory and excellence." He has provided us with tools for crafting an inner self of serenity and beauty within this complexity.

Thank you, my Maker, for creating me wonderfully complex; your workmanship is marvelous.

Delray Agnes

Sweeten Your Life

Throw a tiny party to celebrate how amazing you are because of God. Get a cupcake or a brownie, put on a party hat, and sing a song of joy. God made you, and he thinks you're marvelous!

Girlfriends Gathered 'Round

> God is our merciful Father and the source of all comfort. He comforts us in all our troubles so that we can comfort others. When they are troubled, we will be able to give them the same comfort God has given us.
> (2 Corinthians 1:3-4)

It was March 9 when I stared at the caller ID on my phone. I already knew in my gut what the answer would be, and that when I answered it, I would receive the call every woman dreads. Sure enough, when I answered, my doctor said, "Dianne, your biopsy confirmed it is cancer."

I was scheduled for a mastectomy.

I was new in town, so nearly all my friends were e-mail pals. But there was Eve, who works with my husband. Eve and I had known each other some previously, but since I'd moved to the same town, we were quickly becoming friends. Eve was especially jolted by my diagnosis, since the friend she used to job-share with, Cindy, whom I knew through a Bible study, had died from breast cancer less than a year earlier. Eve was the first to show up at my door, carrying a single pink rose and a gift of a breast cancer ornament. Eve introduced me to two of her friends, Candy and Mary, each of whom had also been through this.

When my friend Kathy, whom I've known since high school, heard of my diagnosis, although she lived half a nation away, she sent her love and a box of fruit. Marie lives several states away, and she sent her love with a handmade necklace that included a pink breast cancer ribbon.

My friend Gayle told me she had her entire church praying for me. Imagine! People I didn't even know were praying for me! I'd never experienced that before. My own church from the previous town where I'd lived also put me on their prayer list. I learned how much I needed those faithful pray-ers. They became precious to me when I couldn't pray for myself during surgery or when my mind was muddled with concerns or when I was too tired to concentrate while recovering.

When church members and other friends were in town, they stopped in to visit. Jan, and Karen and her daughter, stopped by just to talk. They helped me sort out different challenges I was facing. Nadine brought food to go in our freezer and cook as needed.

Every time I turned around, I found I had girlfriends gathering around me, and oh, what a precious blessing they were!

My cancer was caught early by my annual mammogram. It had not spread and so, thankfully, I would not need chemotherapy or radiation. Three more reconstructive surgeries over the next year, doctors promised, would "make me look normal with clothes on."

The following spring, within two days I learned of three friends who received similar diagnoses. Immediately I e-mailed one, called another, and visited the one next door. I baked bread, sent cards, and took gifts. I could offer them the information and knowledge I had gained over the past year, make suggestions, and offer resources.

When hard times hit, girlfriends gather around. It's what we do. It's the way God made us. And it's beautiful.

Dianne Butts

Is there one girlfriend facing a challenge whom you can gather around? Send a card, a note, or a rose. Stop by for a visit. Call and listen. Do you need friends to gather around you? Call someone, and let her know your need.

Chocolate Chess Pie

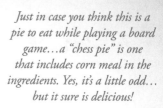

Just in case you think this is a pie to eat while playing a board game…a "chess pie" is one that includes corn meal in the ingredients. Yes, it's a little odd… but it sure is delicious!

Ingredients:

1 cup sugar

3 tablespoons cornmeal

3 tablespoons cocoa

3 eggs, well beaten

½ cup melted butter

½ cup white corn syrup

1 teaspoon vanilla

1 unbaked pie crust

Directions:

Stir the sugar, cornmeal, and cocoa together in a bowl. Add the eggs, butter, corn syrup, and vanilla. Mix well and pour into the unbaked pie shell.

Bake at 350 degrees for 45 minutes.

Cool before serving. Sweet!

Jump!

There are many virtuous and capable women in the world, but you surpass them all!
(Proverbs 31:29)

"No jumping on the bed!"

Isn't that what moms are supposed to say? Well my mom is different. For my 16th birthday my mom, my aunt, and my best friend went to stay at a hotel…and we all jumped on the beds! It was my mom's birthday too (we're extra lucky to share the same birthday!) so it was a memorable celebration.

My mom was a great friend to me when I was 16, and she's still one of my closest friends, along with my aunt and my sisters. I treasure these friendships so much because of the close connection we have being both friends and family.

A few years back my mom, sister, aunt, and I decided we needed to have a few traditions to give us quality time to spend together. We enjoy each other's company so much—it seemed we needed some "excuses" to get together—just the girls. So we decided that we could at least go out to dinner for each of our birthdays. Birthdays don't seem to come around often enough because I'm always looking at the calendar to see when our next dinner out will be. But my birthday is coming up in a few weeks (and Mom's is too!), so I know we'll be getting together soon. I wonder if I can convince everyone to jump on the beds again…Mom? Whaddaya think?

Melissa Towers

Sweeten Your Life

Jump on the bed. Really! No one will tell on you. Jump for joy and for every jump, thank God for a woman in your life. Don't bump your head on the ceiling!

Notes:

_____

_____

_____

_____

_____

_____

_____

_____

_____

_____

_____

_____

_____

_____

_____

_____

_____

_____

_____

_____

_____

God So Loved the World…That He Created Chocolate